German Philosophy: A Very Short Introduction

VERY SHORT INTRODUCTIONS are for anyone wanting a stimulating and accessible way into a new subject. They are written by experts, and have been translated into more than 45 different languages.

The series began in 1995, and now covers a wide variety of topics in every discipline. The VSI library now contains over 500 volumes—a Very Short Introduction to everything from Psychology and Philosophy of Science to American History and Relativity—and continues to grow in every subject area.

Titles in the series include the following:

AFRICAN HISTORY John Parker and Richard Rathbone
AGEING Nancy A. Pachana
ALGEBRA Peter M. Higgins
AMERICAN HISTORY Paul S. Boyer
AMERICAN IMMIGRATION David A. Gerber
AMERICAN LEGAL HISTORY G. Edward White
AMERICAN POLITICAL HISTORY Donald Critchlow
AMERICAN POLITICAL PARTIES AND ELECTIONS L. Sandy Maisel
AMERICAN POLITICS Richard M. Valelly
THE AMERICAN PRESIDENCY Charles O. Jones
AMERICAN SLAVERY Heather Andrea Williams
ANARCHISM Colin Ward
ANCIENT EGYPT Ian Shaw
ANCIENT GREECE Paul Cartledge
THE ANCIENT NEAR EAST Amanda H. Podany
ANCIENT PHILOSOPHY Julia Annas
ANCIENT WARFARE Harry Sidebottom
ANGLICANISM Mark Chapman
THE ANGLO-SAXON AGE John Blair
ANIMAL BEHAVIOUR Tristram D. Wyatt
ANIMAL RIGHTS David DeGrazia
ANXIETY Daniel Freeman and Jason Freeman
ARCHAEOLOGY Paul Bahn
ARISTOTLE Jonathan Barnes
ART HISTORY Dana Arnold
ART THEORY Cynthia Freeland
ASTROPHYSICS James Binney
ATHEISM Julian Baggini
THE ATMOSPHERE Paul I. Palmer
AUGUSTINE Henry Chadwick
BACTERIA Sebastian G. B. Amyes
BARTHES Jonathan Culler
BEAUTY Roger Scruton
THE BIBLE John Riches
BLACK HOLES Katherine Blundell
BLOOD Chris Cooper
THE BRAIN Michael O'Shea
THE BRICS Andrew F. Cooper
BRITISH POLITICS Anthony Wright
BUDDHA Michael Carrithers
BUDDHISM Damien Keown
BUDDHIST ETHICS Damien Keown
BYZANTIUM Peter Sarris
CANCER Nicholas James
CAPITALISM James Fulcher
CATHOLICISM Gerald O'Collins
THE CELTS Barry Cunliffe
CHEMISTRY Peter Atkins
CHOICE THEORY Michael Allingham
CHRISTIANITY Linda Woodhead
CIRCADIAN RHYTHMS Russell Foster and Leon Kreitzman
CITIZENSHIP Richard Bellamy
CLASSICAL MYTHOLOGY Helen Morales
CLASSICS Mary Beard and John Henderson

CLIMATE Mark Maslin
CLIMATE CHANGE Mark Maslin
THE COLD WAR Robert McMahon
COMBINATORICS Robin Wilson
COMMUNISM Leslie Holmes
COMPUTER SCIENCE Subrata Dasgupta
CONSCIOUSNESS Susan Blackmore
CONTEMPORARY ART Julian Stallabrass
CORAL REEFS Charles Sheppard
COSMOLOGY Peter Coles
THE CRUSADES Christopher Tyerman
DADA AND SURREALISM David Hopkins
DANTE Peter Hainsworth and David Robey
DARWIN Jonathan Howard
THE DEAD SEA SCROLLS Timothy Lim
DECOLONIZATION Dane Kennedy
DEMOCRACY Bernard Crick
DESIGN John Heskett
DINOSAURS David Norman
DREAMING J. Allan Hobson
DRUGS Les Iversen
DRUIDS Barry Cunliffe
THE EARTH Martin Redfern
ECONOMICS Partha Dasgupta
EGYPTIAN MYTH Geraldine Pinch
THE ELEMENTS Philip Ball
EMOTION Dylan Evans
EMPIRE Stephen Howe
ENGLISH LITERATURE Jonathan Bate
THE ENLIGHTENMENT John Robertson
EPICUREANISM Catherine Wilson
EPIDEMIOLOGY Rodolfo Saracci
ETHICS Simon Blackburn
EUGENICS Philippa Levine
THE EUROPEAN UNION John Pinder and Simon Usherwood
EVOLUTION Brian and Deborah Charlesworth
EXISTENTIALISM Thomas Flynn
FASCISM Kevin Passmore
FEMINISM Margaret Walters
THE FIRST WORLD WAR Michael Howard
FORENSIC PSYCHOLOGY David Canter
FOUCAULT Gary Gutting
FREE SPEECH Nigel Warburton
FREE WILL Thomas Pink
FREUD Anthony Storr
FUNDAMENTALISM Malise Ruthven
FUNGI Nicholas P. Money
GALAXIES John Gribbin
GALILEO Stillman Drake
GAME THEORY Ken Binmore
GANDHI Bhikhu Parekh
GEOGRAPHY John Matthews and David Herbert
GEOPOLITICS Klaus Dodds
GLOBAL CATASTROPHES Bill McGuire
GLOBAL ECONOMIC HISTORY Robert C. Allen
GLOBALIZATION Manfred Steger
GOD John Bowker
HABERMAS James Gordon Finlayson
HEGEL Peter Singer
HINDUISM Kim Knott
HISTORY John H. Arnold
THE HISTORY OF LIFE Michael Benton
THE HISTORY OF MATHEMATICS Jacqueline Stedall
THE HISTORY OF MEDICINE William Bynum
THE HISTORY OF TIME Leofranc Holford-Strevens
HIV AND AIDS Alan Whiteside
HOLLYWOOD Peter Decherney
HUMAN ANATOMY Leslie Klenerman
HUMAN EVOLUTION Bernard Wood
HUMAN RIGHTS Andrew Clapham
IDEOLOGY Michael Freeden
INDIAN PHILOSOPHY Sue Hamilton
INFINITY Ian Stewart
INFORMATION Luciano Floridi
INNOVATION Mark Dodgson and David Gann
INTELLIGENCE Ian J. Deary
INTERNATIONAL MIGRATION Khalid Koser
INTERNATIONAL RELATIONS Paul Wilkinson
ISLAM Malise Ruthven
ISLAMIC HISTORY Adam Silverstein
JESUS Richard Bauckham
JOURNALISM Ian Hargreaves

JUDAISM Norman Solomon
JUNG Anthony Stevens
KABBALAH Joseph Dan
KANT Roger Scruton
KNOWLEDGE Jennifer Nagel
THE KORAN Michael Cook
LATE ANTIQUITY Gillian Clark
LAW Raymond Wacks
THE LAWS OF THERMODYNAMICS Peter Atkins
LEADERSHIP Keith Grint
LEARNING Mark Haselgrove
LIGHT Ian Walmsley
LINGUISTICS Peter Matthews
LITERARY THEORY Jonathan Culler
LOCKE John Dunn
LOGIC Graham Priest
MACHIAVELLI Quentin Skinner
MARTIN LUTHER Scott H. Hendrix
MARTYRDOM Jolyon Mitchell
MARX Peter Singer
MATHEMATICS Timothy Gowers
THE MEANING OF LIFE Terry Eagleton
MEASUREMENT David Hand
MEDICAL ETHICS Tony Hope
MEDIEVAL BRITAIN John Gillingham and Ralph A. Griffiths
MEDIEVAL LITERATURE Elaine Treharne
MEDIEVAL PHILOSOPHY John Marenbon
MEMORY Jonathan K. Foster
METAPHYSICS Stephen Mumford
MICROSCOPY Terence Allen
MILITARY JUSTICE Eugene R. Fidell
MODERN ART David Cottington
MODERN CHINA Rana Mitter
MODERN IRELAND Senia Pašeta
MODERN ITALY Anna Cento Bull
MODERN JAPAN Christopher Goto-Jones
MODERNISM Christopher Butler
MOLECULAR BIOLOGY Aysha Divan and Janice A. Royds
MOLECULES Philip Ball
MOONS David A. Rothery
MUSIC Nicholas Cook
MYTH Robert A. Segal
NEOLIBERALISM Manfred Steger and Ravi Roy
NEWTON Robert Iliffe
NIETZSCHE Michael Tanner
NORTH AMERICAN INDIANS Theda Perdue and Michael D. Green
NORTHERN IRELAND Marc Mulholland
NOTHING Frank Close
NUCLEAR PHYSICS Frank Close
NUTRITION David A. Bender
THE PALESTINIAN-ISRAELI CONFLICT Martin Bunton
PANDEMICS Christian W. McMillen
PARTICLE PHYSICS Frank Close
THE PERIODIC TABLE Eric R. Scerri
PHILOSOPHY Edward Craig
PHILOSOPHY IN THE ISLAMIC WORLD Peter Adamson
PHILOSOPHY OF LAW Raymond Wacks
PHILOSOPHY OF SCIENCE Samir Okasha
PHOTOGRAPHY Steve Edwards
PHYSICAL CHEMISTRY Peter Atkins
PLANETS David A. Rothery
PLATO Julia Annas
POLITICAL PHILOSOPHY David Miller
POLITICS Kenneth Minogue
POPULISM Cas Mudde and Cristóbal Rovira Kaltwasser
POSTCOLONIALISM Robert Young
POSTMODERNISM Christopher Butler
POSTSTRUCTURALISM Catherine Belsey
PREHISTORY Chris Gosden
PRESOCRATIC PHILOSOPHY Catherine Osborne
PSYCHIATRY Tom Burns
PSYCHOLOGY Gillian Butler and Freda McManus
PSYCHOTHERAPY Tom Burns and Eva Burns-Lundgren
PUBLIC HEALTH Virginia Berridge
QUANTUM THEORY John Polkinghorne
RACISM Ali Rattansi
THE REFORMATION Peter Marshall
RELATIVITY Russell Stannard
THE RENAISSANCE Jerry Brotton
RENAISSANCE ART Geraldine A. Johnson

REVOLUTIONS Jack A. Goldstone
RHETORIC Richard Toye
RISK Baruch Fischhoff and John Kadvany
RITUAL Barry Stephenson
RIVERS Nick Middleton
ROBOTICS Alan Winfield
ROMAN BRITAIN Peter Salway
THE ROMAN EMPIRE Christopher Kelly
THE ROMAN REPUBLIC David M. Gwynn
RUSSIAN HISTORY Geoffrey Hosking
THE RUSSIAN REVOLUTION S. A. Smith
SCHIZOPHRENIA Chris Frith and Eve Johnstone
SCIENCE AND RELIGION Thomas Dixon
SEXUALITY Véronique Mottier
SHAKESPEARE'S COMEDIES Bart van Es
SIKHISM Eleanor Nesbitt
SLEEP Steven W. Lockley and Russell G. Foster
SOCIAL AND CULTURAL ANTHROPOLOGY John Monaghan and Peter Just
SOCIAL PSYCHOLOGY Richard J. Crisp
SOCIAL WORK Sally Holland and Jonathan Scourfield
SOCIALISM Michael Newman
SOCIOLOGY Steve Bruce
SOCRATES C. C. W. Taylor
SOUND Mike Goldsmith
THE SOVIET UNION Stephen Lovell
THE SPANISH CIVIL WAR Helen Graham
SPANISH LITERATURE Jo Labanyi
STATISTICS David J. Hand
STUART BRITAIN John Morrill
SYMMETRY Ian Stewart
TAXATION Stephen Smith
TELESCOPES Geoff Cottrell
TERRORISM Charles Townshend
THEOLOGY David F. Ford
TIBETAN BUDDHISM Matthew T. Kapstein
THE TROJAN WAR Eric H. Cline
THE TUDORS John Guy
THE UNITED NATIONS Jussi M. Hanhimäki
THE U.S. CONGRESS Donald A. Ritchie
THE U.S. SUPREME COURT Linda Greenhouse
THE VIKINGS Julian Richards
VIRUSES Dorothy H. Crawford
WAR AND TECHNOLOGY Alex Roland
WILLIAM SHAKESPEARE Stanley Wells
WITCHCRAFT Malcolm Gaskill
THE WORLD TRADE ORGANIZATION Amrita Narlikar
WORLD WAR II Gerhard L. Weinberg

Andrew Bowie

GERMAN PHILOSOPHY

A Very Short Introduction

OXFORD
UNIVERSITY PRESS

Great Clarendon Street, Oxford OX2 6DP

Oxford University Press is a department of the University of Oxford.
It furthers the University's objective of excellence in research, scholarship,
and education by publishing worldwide in

Oxford New York

Auckland Cape Town Dar es Salaam Hong Kong Karachi
Kuala Lumpur Madrid Melbourne Mexico City Nairobi
New Delhi Shanghai Taipei Toronto

With offices in

Argentina Austria Brazil Chile Czech Republic France Greece
Guatemala Hungary Italy Japan Poland Portugal Singapore
South Korea Switzerland Thailand Turkey Ukraine Vietnam

Oxford is a registered trade mark of Oxford University Press
in the UK and in certain other countries

Published in the United States
by Oxford University Press Inc., New York

First published 2010

British Library Cataloguing in Publication Data
Data available

Library of Congress Cataloging in Publication Data
Data available

Typeset by SPI Publisher Services, Pondicherry, India

Printed and bound by
CPI Group (UK) Ltd, Croydon, CR0 4YY

ISBN 978-0-19-956925-0

Contents

List of illustrations

Introduction: why German philosophy?

German philosophy has a sometimes deserved reputation for being both impenetrable and excessively speculative, and much of it effectively disappeared from view in the Anglo-American philosophical world from the 1930s to the 1970s. This disappearance was based in part on the suspicion that Nazism and German philosophy might somehow be complicit with each other. It is only recently that there has been a substantial revival of interest in such figures as G. W. F. Hegel and Martin Heidegger in the Anglo-American philosophical world. The growth of interest, not just within academic philosophy, in German philosophy has to do with a widespread sense of crisis with respect to the direction of the contemporary world. The crisis relates to key factors in what is often termed 'modernity'. Modernity emerges in different societies at different times, but it generally involves certain characteristic features. Societies prior to modernity tend to rely on a traditional, theologically underpinned world-picture. Even though that picture involves tensions that sometimes lead to violence and social disruption, it still forms a largely stable background to how people respond to the world. Modernity, in contrast, forces cultures to confront the results of the rise of the modern natural sciences and of new forms of production and exchange. The threat to the certainties of the old order often has traumatic effects, making many people cling to rigid conceptions of that order. They oppose the changes which the new order involves, even as they employ much that those changes bring about. The move to a more stable new order only proves possible after catastrophic events make the move an inescapable necessity.

Aspects of this story could be applied to some of the contemporary Islamic world's ambivalence with regard to modern Western culture, but it is the often disastrous course of German history from the 17th century until the end of the Second World War and the eventual fall of the Berlin Wall in 1989 which offers perhaps the most graphic version of how the transition to modernity can occur. German philosophy is significantly two-edged with regard to this transition: it is both a problematic symptom of German history, and a vital resource for trying to see how one might come to terms with a world in which, as Karl Marx put it in the *Communist Manifesto* of 1848, 'Everything established and solid melts into air, everything holy is desecrated, and people are finally forced to see their place in life, their relationships in the sober light of day'. The two-edged nature of German philosophy can, therefore, be valuable for addressing dilemmas in the contemporary world. Recent events make it clear that in many quarters the need for religion has not disappeared, even though science has undermined many of the ideas which traditionally sustained religion, and consumerism increasingly undermines many of the religious values of traditional societies. The tension between needs formerly catered for by religion and the social effects of modern science and modern capitalism is a key to much of German philosophy.

Those who are used to the terms of reference of Anglo-American 'analytical philosophy' may think such claims are irrelevant to their concerns. However, analytical philosophy suggests by its very name that it is itself a manifestation of modernity. One source of the success of the modern natural sciences is precisely the concentration on the analysis of objects into their constituent elements and the formulation of laws governing those elements. An analytical approach to philosophy similarly began by seeking to isolate the elements of language by abstracting them from their relations to other phenomena and trying to establish general rules which govern them. The goal was a theory of truth and meaning based on showing how words and sentences connect to the bits of reality to which they refer. A general account of how language works was to be derived from analysis of its particular elements. The aim was to answer or dissolve many of the traditional problems of philosophy, by showing how they were the result of the logical inadequacy of everyday forms of language.

It is now widely thought that this approach will be unable to achieve its aim. Meaning cannot be assumed to be fully analysable in a piecemeal fashion, and the idea of a logically purified language always relies on prior understanding of 'impure' natural languages. The ways in which language's elements relate to each other, and non-linguistic practices and background knowledge that are not inherent in the elements of language are essential to accounting for meaning. The focus of philosophy consequently shifts from a concentration on how language 'represents' things, to a focus on all the ways in which language 'expresses' or 'articulates' how we relate to the world. The latter can range from objective statements about what we know, to expressions of our existence in both verbal and non-verbal forms, such as music or painting. This 'holistic' conception has been a part of German philosophy since the second half of the 18th century, and it is in the German tradition that many of the key alternatives to an analytical approach to philosophy can be sought. The contrast between analytical and holistic conceptions also relates to contrasting cultural attitudes. Whereas the analytical tradition's orientation is predominantly towards the natural sciences, the German tradition attaches great importance to art and to aesthetic issues.

This contrast suggests a crucial tension within modern philosophy. The tension can be characterized in a variety of ways, such as between 'explanation' and 'understanding', or 'positivism' and 'Romanticism', or the 'two cultures' of the sciences and the humanities. How do we deal, as in many situations we must, with clashes between the way science tells us the world is, and the other ways in which people interpret and feel about their world? German philosophy begins in earnest when the sense is put in question that humankind is 'at home' in a world whose intelligibility is underwritten by God. One consequence of this change is that competing ways of interpreting the world seem to become irreconcilable, generating precisely the kind of conflicts characteristic of modernity.

This issue has not gone away, as the following can suggest. In the last 30 years or so, the study of the humanities has seen the emergence of a growing number of highly contested theoretical approaches. These have, in particular, involved interrogating received ideas about meaning and truth. This questioning caught on in part because the narrow and ethnocentric assumptions on which the judgement of culture in the Western world too often relied have been shaken by the effects of globalization and the decline of colonialism. The awareness that culture is always connected to the workings of power, and that what is held as true is deeply affected by historical circumstance means that understanding culture demands theoretically informed reflection. The theoretical approaches that have changed the humanities in controversial ways, of which the most familiar are structuralism, post-structuralism, gender theory, critical theory, hermeneutics, and psychoanalysis, have, though, not tended to include analytical philosophy. What is sometimes forgotten or ignored is that most of these theoretical approaches, which are often associated with French theorists like Jacques Derrida, Michel Foucault, and others, depend upon the key figures in German philosophy, most notably Hegel, Nietzsche, and Heidegger. It is now precisely the ideas of these latter figures which are also being used to challenge some of the assumptions of Anglo-American analytical philosophy. Attention to German philosophy therefore offers opportunities for new interactions between previously opposed approaches.

The main aim here is, though, to explore what German philosophy tells us about some of the major problems of modernity. This approach should make it easier for readers then to engage with the admittedly difficult major texts of German philosophy, which have been so important in establishing the terms in which the modern world can be understood. A more detailed account of the philosophical arguments is offered in my *Introduction to German Philosophy from Kant to Habermas* (Cambridge: Polity, 2003).

Chapter 1
Kant and modernity

Why is Kant so important?

Anyone reading the works of Immanuel Kant (1724–1804) is faced with a barrage of technical terms, such as 'synthetic judgements a priori' and 'transcendental unity of apperception'. How does one get from trying to understand these terms to the fact that Kant is central to any account, both of how philosophy changes in the modern world, and of how philosophy can change the modern world? The answer is that Kant's philosophy has to be grasped as part of the larger historical picture of which it is an expression. Even if we are unsure about the validity or the meaning of his ideas, we can still read his work as a response to revolutionary changes in the world of his time. The implicit tension here, between the idea that we should establish the truth about Kant's philosophy, and the idea that we should understand him as an expression of his era, itself becomes an issue in the period in which Kant is writing. This is because the assumption that things have a timeless, rational essence is put in question by a new philosophical focus on how human practices affect the ways in which the world is understood. The new focus is both affected by and affects the rapid social, political, economic, and scientific transformations in the period from the second half of the 18th century onwards in Europe.

Kant's relationship to these transformations is not straightforward – he lived most of his life away from the centre of things in Königsberg, in East Prussia – but they must inform his work. If his reflections on freedom, for example, have nothing to do with the French Revolution, it is hard to know how we should think about them concretely at all. Judgements on those reflections should not, though, just depend on the contexts in which they emerged, and this means that philosophy seems to involve contradictory demands. We should, however, not necessarily try to conjure away such philosophical contradictions, because they can be expressions of tensions in social and political life which cannot be resolved by philosophy itself. In seeking to resolve some of the most important philosophical dilemmas of his era, then, Kant takes us beyond those dilemmas into wider problems of the modern world.

The philosophical context

The positions to which Kant responds are themselves expressions of historical factors that are central to modernity. The 'Rationalism' of Gottfried Leibniz (1646–1716) and Baruch Spinoza (1632–77), which is carried on by Christian Wolff (1679–1754) and others into Kant's era, assumes that the new success of mathematically founded natural science is based on structures inherent in nature. Because mathematics consists of necessary truths which cannot be changed by empirical evidence, it can have a foundational status lacking in any other form of knowledge. Its absolute status seems also to connect it to theology: empirical knowledge is necessarily fallible, so the infallibility of mathematics can be regarded as having a source beyond the human. However, as the Scottish philosopher David Hume (1711–76) suggested, the modern sciences also depend on a new, close attention to empirical data. These data are derived from human perceptions, so they have none of the necessity of mathematics. Hume's claims had the effect on Kant of awakening him from his 'dogmatic' faith in the idea of an inbuilt cosmic order: for Kant, 'dogmatism' is the

1. Immanuel Kant, c. 1790

belief, present in philosophy at least since Plato, in fundamental metaphysical principles which are not themselves subjected to critical examination. For Hume, the principle of causality cannot be said to be built into the universe because all the evidence for causal necessity derives from our perception of one thing following another. Any apparent certainty generated by the new sciences is therefore accompanied by uncertainty about what legitimates that certainty. The implications for religion of Hume's view are potentially disastrous: the order of things now depends on whatever it is that individual human beings happen to perceive, not on divine authority.

Kant seeks a resolution to the clash between rationalism and empiricism by rethinking the relationship between mathematical necessity and contingent perceptions. He is not, though, just concerned with epistemology. His first major work, the *Critique of Pure Reason* (1781, second edition 1787), already makes freedom a central concern, which he then develops in the 'second Critique', the *Critique of Practical Reason* (1788) (and in the *Foundation of the Metaphysics of Morals* (1785)). In 1790, Kant published his 'third Critique', the *Critique of Judgement* (1790), which deals with the issue of teleology (the idea that there is design or purpose in nature), and with natural and artistic beauty.

How, then, do the differing issues that Kant confronts relate to each other? Modern science becomes the preserve of increasingly specialized scientific disciplines: one consequence of this is that analysis of nature into specific components can give rise to a sense of disintegration. Previous philosophy and theology had assumed an underlying unity in the diversity of natural phenomena, and Hume makes the source of this unity into a major philosophical problem. Kant therefore attempts to establish new forms of unity to replace those which are no longer sustainable. He is, though, not just concerned with scientific knowledge, but also with the moral basis of society, and with relationships to nature that cannot be explained by scientific laws. The three Critiques can be seen as expressions of how the domains of science, of law and morality, and of art, become more distinct from each other in the modern period, even as their relationships to each other become a vital concern.

'Transcendental idealism'

In Kant's day, 'idealism' was associated with Bishop Berkeley's notion that 'being is perceiving': unless something is perceived, how can we assert that it exists at all? Kant insists, however, that his 'transcendental' idealism is actually a kind of 'realism', because it assumes that objects do exist independently of our perceptions. He may therefore seem to be involved in paradoxical or contradictory stances. This impression is reinforced by the fact that the aim of transcendental idealism is to give a basis for *objectivity* in terms of *subjectivity*. The objective necessities of the laws of nature depend upon subjective 'conditions of possibility' of knowledge: these conditions are what is meant by the 'transcendental' aspect of his epistemology. The conditions are subjective, because they are functions of our thinking, but they must involve necessity, rather than being arbitrary in the manner of subjective opinions. Kant wants, therefore, to explain how knowledge – he takes Newton's laws of motion as the paradigm case – depends both on the impact of the world on us and on the ways in which the mind orders that impact.

The underlying problem is that what belongs on the subject-side and what belongs on the object-side of knowledge is (and remains) one of the most contested issues in modern philosophy. Some philosophers these days think, for example, that the brain is a piece of hardware that runs the software necessary for thought, so that the software can also be instantiated by the mechanisms of a computer. In these terms, the subjective side of knowledge can therefore be explained causally. On the other hand, 'intentionality', the fact that thinking is 'about' things, suggests that what apprehends a world of objects cannot itself be an object in the same way as the objects it apprehends. This is crucial for Kant. The intentional aspect allows us to produce different judgements about something, which can be 'seen as' a potentially endless number of things. Whatever the truth of the philosophical arguments here, the stances taken with regard to them affect how human beings think about themselves.

Why, then, is Kant led to the doctrine of transcendental idealism at all? The reason is implicit in his dictum that 'Thoughts without content are empty; intuitions without concepts are blind'. The former are ('dogmatic') thoughts such as those about the nature of God based just on the concepts which have been used to talk about God, like 'necessary existence', 'perfection', and so on. 'Intuitions' – the German word is '*Anschauungen*', which comes from '*anschauen*', 'to look at' – are the material of our perceptions that can be used as justificatory evidence. Without ways of organizing evidence by identifying it in terms of concepts, one would be faced with endless chaotic particularity: what we perceive is always different from moment to moment in some, however minimal, respect, and no two objects are absolutely identical. Although Kant wishes to keep what he proposes separate from psychology, psychological research into perception proves how much what we see is structured by the conceptual structures we already possess. Despite the problems concerning the relationship between the data of perception and our thinking, Kant does not doubt that scientific knowledge is possible, so the task is to say what makes it possible. Sameness is not something encountered in the world of perceptual data, which can never be shown to be completely identical and occur at specific places and times. Transcendental idealism therefore claims that there must be mental rules for apprehending the world, such that objects must follow our ways of thinking, rather than vice versa. Kant saw this change of perspective as a 'Copernican turn', analogous to Copernicus's turning Ptolemaic cosmology inside-out by arguing that the Earth is not the centre of the universe.

Kant calls the general rules for apprehending objects 'categories', a term he derives from Aristotle, who saw categories as defining the ways in which things can be said to be. For Kant, categories specify 'concepts of an object in general', which cannot be derived from looking at the world. The categories of oneness and manyness are the basis of what Kant terms 'synthetic judgements a priori'. These are mathematical judgements which had previously been thought to be a priori, but which Kant thinks prove how the mind could add to its knowledge while thinking in pure terms. The number 4 cannot be defined, say, just as 2 + 2, because it can also be the synthesis of 3 and 1, 4 and 0, and an infinity of other combinations, such as 3.3333 and 0.6667, all of which can add to our knowledge of 4. (A still disputed issue is whether all these combinations are to be thought of as already 'contained in' 4, even if we don't calculate them.) The category of causality offers the best way to understand his overall argument. If I think something causes something else, I will judge that event *b* necessarily follows event *a*. What I perceive is *a* and then *b*: thinking of them as causally connected requires more than the succession of one event by another. It requires both the category of cause, and the ability to judge that the connection of *b* to the preceding *a* is a necessary one. Judgement actively synthesizes different bits of perceptual experience into a relationship with each other. Kant sees judgements as 'spontaneous': they are not, unlike everything in the world of nature, caused by something else. Judgements involve us actively taking a stance on whether something is the case or not. The material of cognition is given to us by passive 'receptivity', and knowledge results from the active application of categories and concepts to that material. Perhaps surprisingly (and questionably), Kant insists that space and time are a framework provided by our thinking, rather than properties of the objective world. This is because we only ever apprehend things at a specific place and time, there being no way of apprehending things 'all at once'. The need for synthesis comes about because experience happens within this limiting framework: thinking has to connect different moments of experience to make them intelligible.

The modern subject

The whole edifice of Kant's account of knowledge depends on what he calls the 'synthetic unity of apperception'. 'Apperception' is the ability to reflect on one's judgements: I can apperceive this afternoon the fact that I thought about my holidays this morning. I must therefore have existed both at the moment of thinking about my holidays and at the moment of thinking about thinking about them. This 'synthetic' continuity of myself is the basis of memory. Without what connects the moments of experience, which must logically be the same at both moments, there is no way of bringing together what is different. Kant therefore says that 'an "*I think*" must *be able* to accompany all my representations'. The logical point can, though, involve something more emphatic: the very idea of a coherent world now seems to depend on the unity of the subject. This unity can therefore be thought of in two ways. The first involves only the logical point just outlined. In the second, the unity can be inflated into the idea of the self as the 'light' which makes the universe intelligible. This ambivalent status of the self becomes very important in subsequent German philosophy.

Modernity involves a huge increase in the human capacity to gain knowledge and control of nature. If the basis of this capacity is indeed the activity of the subject, the problems brought about by scientific and technological changes can be related to different interpretations of subjectivity. Because it is finite and mortal, the subject is inherently dependent on its being a natural being; at the same time, it can also dominate more and more of both external and internal nature. The domination of nature may then lead to disastrous attempts to overcome the subject's dependence on nature. Moreover, the subject seems at the same time both to be part of physical nature, and yet also not part of nature, because it has the moral freedom to withstand natural urges. Kant confronts the ambiguities that arise from this dual status. The contradictory ways in which he has been interpreted can therefore be read as expressions of the divided nature of humankind's view of itself in modernity.

'Things in themselves'

The sense of the divisions in modern human existence is most apparent in Kant's reflections on freedom. These depend on his distinction between how the world appears and how the world is 'in itself', between the world as 'phenomenon' and the world as 'noumenon'. Everything in the appearing world is subject to deterministic laws, including, therefore, our own brains and the rest of our bodies. At the same time, when we resist the causally explicable promptings of our instincts, we are acting in terms of a 'causality through freedom'. We cause ourselves not to do something because we think it is wrong. The implausible side of Kant's view lies in the fact that such decisions therefore do not take place in space and time, because everything that does is subject to deterministic laws. The plausible side of this view is reflected in the fact that societies hold their members responsible for what they do, unless it can be shown that they were caused to do it by forces beyond their control.

Kant sees us as free 'in ourselves', but as determined by natural laws *qua* appearing objects in nature. The meaning of a 'thing in itself' is, though, notoriously ambiguous. We cannot perceive all of an object at once, so it might mean the totality of the aspects of an object. It could, though, also mean that the real nature of things is constitutively hidden, because we only have access to things 'for us'. This ambiguity indicates a modern sense of unease about the place of humankind in nature. Nature may be potentially, if not actually, accessible in all its aspects to human knowledge. However, it could also be that scientific knowledge obscures or occasions ways in which we fail to understand nature. Some of the most important human relationships to nature do not depend on knowledge of causal laws. They may have to do, for example, with how nature can be a resource for spiritual renewal, or be something to be protected against the depredations of technology. Ideas like these arise because there seems to be a connection between human freedom and the sense of an unknowable side to nature: neither freedom nor nature in itself are part of the world of appearances.

Reason and freedom

Kant is aware that one cannot simply conjure away the issues raised by 'metaphysics', the establishing of a general picture of how the world is constituted. The task of 'reason', as opposed to that of cognitive 'understanding', is to establish principles that make our thoughts coherent. Discovering ever more new laws of nature does not tell us about how those laws relate to each other. For that, one needs the 'idea' that all natural phenomena are law-bound and constitute an overall system, which is not something we can know is the case. Ideas have a 'regulative' status: we need them to order thoughts about things in general, but what they claim is not 'constitutive', because that would involve a claim of the kind Kant rejects as 'dogmatic'. All questions about the ultimate nature of things therefore become unanswerable, but this does not, as Kant himself insists, get rid of the impulse to ask them.

In the first Critique, Kant, who is himself a believer, devastatingly proves that the existing philosophical proofs that God exists are invalid. Religion must therefore be a matter of faith, not knowledge. So where does that leave the 'big' questions about the meaning of life? The austerity of some of what Kant has to offer here is a result of the restrictions we have observed. The second Critique and the *Foundation of the Metaphysics of Morals* are attempts to give a basis for morality without appeals to divine authority. The still commonly held belief that morality needs an absolute foundation of the kind provided by theology is not necessarily compelling. Perhaps all I need to prompt me to act morally is the awareness that other people can suffer as I can. Kant, though, remains concerned to give a definitive justification for the criteria one uses to judge what one should do, not least because he sees the need to have ways of justifying legal sanctions on those who do not accept the demand to act morally. The striking thing about what he proposes is that it does not involve concrete moral commandments.

Kant famously maintains that only a 'good will' can be regarded as good without qualification. Anything we regard as good in the empirical world can, in other circumstances, turn out to be bad. The will is located outside nature, where everything is caused by and is the cause of something else. The goodness of a good will does not, however, give any direction with regard to what we should actually do. What we do depends on 'imperatives'. If we wish to achieve a goal, we have to will the means for achieving that goal. This involves 'hypothetical' imperatives, but these have no necessary moral content, because they could include willing the means to kill someone. Morality depends instead on the 'categorical imperative': 'I ought never to act except in such a way *that I can also will that my maxim should become a universal law*'. Kant does not dictate what the maxim (the principle) of my action should be, and this is the crux. The individual has to decide the basis for their actions, rather than have it imposed on them, otherwise they lack what differentiates what we do from what happens in the world of nature. Autonomy does not consist in the ability to do whatever one wishes (and so, as Rousseau argued, be the slave of one's passions), but rather in the ability to act in terms of principles chosen on the assumption that we should not grant to ourselves what we would not grant to others.

Kant's strategy is to point to ways that we acknowledge our common humanity, such as sharing the capacity to be self-governing in terms of principles not dictated by self-interest. This might seem rather naïve: how do we know whether we really are acting autonomously or not, given our capacity for self-deception? Kant accepts that we cannot know this. All he can appeal to is a sense that we have 'the idea of another and much more worthy purpose of existence' than what is governed by natural causality. This idea can lead us to realize that other rational beings should not be just the means to our ends. Rational beings have intrinsic value, a 'dignity', which is beyond 'price', because they are not exchangeable for something else.

Modernity is marked by exploitation, ethnically inspired mass murder, and almost continual warfare, which can make Kant's appeals to a common humanity appear naïve. Hegel will criticize the categorical imperative for lacking any roots in the moral habits and practices which develop in actual historical communities. Kant's demands for universality have, though, not been rendered redundant by such criticisms. Without the demand for a universal idea of humanity, international law lacks a grounding principle. In the wake of the Nazis, the idea of a 'crime against humanity' became essential to international law. Of course, the implementation of international law can be desperately difficult. However, part of Kant's point in separating the empirical world from the realm of freedom is to keep alive the idea that how things ought to be can never be reduced to how they have been. His stance is often criticized from a philosophical point of view, because this separation requires the idea of an 'intelligible' realm of freedom that is outside space and time. However, the philosophical problem of establishing an agreed theory on such matters has not destroyed the idea of humanity as possessing equal rights, based on a notion of the human potential for autonomy.

Nature, beauty, and freedom

Kant both reveals difficulties and suggests new possibilities concerning how humanity relates to nature. If nature is God's creation, the limitations of our knowledge have to do with human finitude and fallibility, and complete knowledge is assumed to reside with the deity. Other responses to nature, such as aesthetic ones, therefore depend on the idea that nature's wonders and mysteries have to do with its divine origin, as suggested in the idea of the 'book of nature'. If such theological conceptions no longer have any philosophical support, humankind's relationship to nature becomes a problem. In the first Critique, nature is just a system of necessary laws. Questions about nature's further significances cannot arise here because all we can say about nature depends on the application of categories and concepts to intuitions. Recent 'materialist' or 'physicalist' philosophical conceptions similarly restrict valid explanations to those provided by the sciences: phenomena which seem to be outside scientific explanation, such as consciousness or aesthetic pleasure, will eventually receive law-bound explanations.

One reason why Kant does not adopt this kind of reductive view is that even notionally complete knowledge of nature does not establish the *point* of that knowledge. What is the point of a wholly objectified view of existence for real human beings in concrete life situations? In the first two Critiques, Kant radically separates the cognitive from the ethical, and this leads to the worry that nature is indeed just a law-bound machine. The modern idea of 'nihilism', the consequence of the idea that there is no value in anything that happens in nature, because it is nothing but chains of causes of other causes, originates here. Before Kant, such concerns did not become urgent because things in nature were assumed to have a goal, a 'telos', towards which they developed. Positive claims about teleology in nature are 'dogmatic', because they cannot be legitimated as knowledge, but Kant is unwilling wholly to give up on teleology. His way of trying to sustain it in the third Critique is still controversial: he connects teleology to natural and artistic beauty.

Although his position here is highly problematic, it is another important historical expression of a change in the way people interpret the world. During the second half of the 18th century, appreciation of the beauty of nature undergoes a radical transformation in the Western world. From being seen as a threat, wild nature, such as the Alps, comes to be seen as a valuable resource, precisely because we cannot control it. Nature becomes a value in itself, and other relationships to nature than the cognitive or theological become significant. This change is part of what inaugurates modern aesthetics. Kant connects the intrinsic beauty of the natural world both to artistic beauty and to non-cognitive responses to nature. The form of a natural object is not something explained by the physical and chemical laws governing it, because it depends on the interrelation of the different constituents of the object. Kant claims that the organic coherence of things in nature means that it is 'as if an understanding contained the basis of the unity of the multiplicity of [nature's] empirical laws'. This is a covertly theological way of sustaining teleology, though Kant admits that one cannot know if there is such an 'understanding'. What is less questionable is his suggestion that the pleasure to be gained from contemplation of the form of organisms in nature compels us to think in terms which are not reducible to scientific laws.

The aim of the *Critique of Judgement* is to investigate how judgement functions 'according to the principle of the appropriateness of nature to our capacity for cognition'. The Critique is therefore meant to provide a principle of unity of humankind and nature that is lacking in the first two Critiques. The principle allows us to grasp the whole of a natural object, rather than merely analyse its parts, and is manifest in our pleasure in the form of natural objects. This idea is linked both to our ability to move from the apprehension of particulars to the formulation of rules governing those particulars, and to the idea that appreciation of art is not merely subjective. Whereas preference for one kind of wine over another comes down to what is 'agreeable' to me or to you, judgements about beauty involve the claim that others should assent to the same judgement. Kant thinks that such potential agreement points to an underlying 'common sense' (*sensus communis*) which enables us to share a world that is intelligible to each of us in the same way: the cognitive and the aesthetic here become inseparable.

Central to Kant's conception is the notion of an 'aesthetic idea', 'that representation of the imagination which gives much to think about, but without any determinate thought, i.e. *concept* being able to be adequate to it'. Such ideas symbolize what is otherwise inaccessible to knowledge, like the idea of goodness. Access to the highest ideas, which point to a shared human sense of value, is non-conceptual, because it does not involve the application of a rule to an intuition. Similarly, in our experience of the 'sublime', when we contemplate threatening natural phenomena, such as lightning, volcanoes, hurricanes, from a position of safety, we get the sense of another way of relating to nature which is not determined by what we can know. Nature here overwhelms our capacity to grasp it, and Kant maintains that the idea of freedom is manifest in our sense of the limits of what we can rationally and empirically grasp.

Kant can seem to be an overly rationalistic philosopher, who leaves too little space for the concerns that give meaning to people's lives. However, in establishing limits on what philosophy can justifiably claim, he is also pushed towards what goes beyond those limits. The significance of the ideas to be examined in the coming chapters lies in how they help us to understand what become the dominant goals of the modern world. The decline of the idea that the most important goals are inherent in the order of the world itself means that the task of establishing goals falls explicitly to ourselves. The great ideological battles in the period around the French Revolution, which lead both to the development of modern democracy, and to the disasters of modernity exemplified by Nazism and Stalinism, are closely linked to the philosophical story which we have seen begin with Kant's insistence on human autonomy.

Chapter 2
The linguistic turn

The missing dimension

Kant offers such a profound new vision of philosophy that it is surprising to realize that he largely ignores a major concern of modern philosophy. Karl Leonhard Reinhold (1757–1823), who was mainly responsible for the initial growth of interest in Kantian philosophy that led to German Idealism (see Chapter 3), remarked in 1812 that 'the relation of thinking to speaking and the character of linguistic usage in philosophizing in no way came under scrutiny and to formulation' in Kant and German Idealism. However, even before Kant wrote his most important texts, there were philosophers in Germany for whom language was crucial. What made these thinkers concentrate on language, when others appear not have considered language to be decisive at all?

Kant argued that the knowable order of the world depends on the cognitive activity of the subject. The contrasting interpretations of that activity are further complicated once language's relationship to subjectivity is considered. Even though subjects manipulate their language, they do not invent it, and in some still disputed sense they need language to become subjects at all. So what is the origin of language? Like the order of the world, language's origin had generally been assumed to be divine. This assumption connected the idea of language as part of God's creation to the intelligibility of the world: the Greek word '*logos*' refers both to the 'word', in the sense of speech, and to the rational order of things. The beginning of modernity in philosophy can be characterized by the near simultaneity of Hume's and Kant's new philosophical questions with questioning of the divine origin of language. The former lead to the idea of the subject as the new centre of philosophy; the latter, in contrast, reveals the subject's dependence on something it does not originate. Language becomes the 'Other', whose origin continues even today to pose significant problems. (Think of the controversies over whether language can be adequately explained in terms of genes.) German philosophy is marked by tensions between approaches which put the subject at the centre of philosophy, and approaches which suggest that the subject is dependent on something other than itself. The idea of this dependence suggests why the notion of 'the unconscious' develops at this time, and the theoretical issues here are once again indications of historical changes. The notion of 'ideology' combines the issues of language and of the unconscious. It emerges during the French Revolution, and initially just meant a system of ideas. 'Ideology' soon develops, though, particularly via Marx, into a term used to characterize people's belief that their actions are self-determined, when they are in fact unconsciously dependent on the dominant ways of speaking and acting of their social class.

A further indication of what is at issue here is the emergence in the second half of the 18th century of the discipline of 'anthropology'. Part of what leads to anthropology is the awareness that the natural language of a people is not just a means of saying the same things as can be said in another language. The language of a people is rather also the product of their particular encounters with the world. Understanding these encounters leads to a new awareness of how different the world may be for other cultures. The importance of this is suggested by cases where the language of an ethnic minority can become crucial to its identity. This kind of identity can, though, often be two-edged. What connects some people can also be what separates them from others, when non-members of a linguistic community become the alien 'Other'. Questions of linguistic identity are also related to the emergence of nationalism, which is a source of so much bloodshed in modern history. It is perhaps for this reason that Johann Gottfried Herder (1744–1803) has sometimes been regarded with – largely unwarranted – suspicion, because of his concentration on the identity-forming role of language.

Representation and expression

Herder, who was a favourite pupil of Kant until they fell out in the 1780s, and his contemporary and friend, Johann Georg Hamann (1730–88), reveal a paradox in modern conceptions of language. As we saw, the new success of the natural sciences is accompanied by doubts about the foundation of that success. In a rationalist view, differences between languages are surmountable because the truths of science can potentially be formulated in any natural language. The rationalist view can therefore seem compatible with conceptions of a God-given order of the universe. However, 18th-century rationalism's appeal to the idea of a 'universal language' is made just as the mathematically based science that helps to lead to this idea is actually undermining many of the previous foundations of theology. The new approaches to language at issue here, on the other hand, question the idea that all languages could, or should, be made commensurable.

Rationalist views tend to regard language primarily in terms of how it 'represents' things in the world. The aim of science is ultimately to arrive at the words which give the true re-presentation – in the sense of that which 'presents again what is already there as such' – of the world. Hamann and Herder argue, in the wake of J.-J. Rousseau and others, that this approach fails to appreciate how language is an essential expression of what it is to be human. Language does far more than just represent the world: it can make new aspects of ourselves and the world manifest that could not be manifest without it. All human symbolic forms, including music and visual art, can therefore be understood as 'language'.

Language and reason

In *On Recent German Literature: Fragments* of 1766–8, Herder already announces what will be the basic premise of 20th-century analytical philosophy: 'If it is true that we cannot think without thoughts and that we learn to think through words: then language gives the whole of human knowledge its limits and outline', and is 'the tool, the content and the form of human thoughts'. The question is how exactly we conceive of language: even today, the differences between analytical and 'continental/European' philosophy are often based on different construals of what language *is*. In an prophetic move, Hamann suggests that language can affect the assessment of Kant's transcendental philosophy. He asks how Kant's categories relate to language, suggesting that 'words are both pure and empirical *intuitions* as well as pure and empirical *concepts*', and his questioning of Kant's separation of receptive intuitions and spontaneous concepts is part of what inaugurates German Idealism.

A central aim of German Idealism is to overcome Kant's oppositions between appearances and things in themselves, and between receptivity and spontaneity. Hamann's point is that we acquire words receptively as noises or marks in the objective world, but that they are not just objects. Words can only *be* words, rather than just marks or noises, if they have a meaning that affects how we understand the world. It might seem obvious that the next thing to do is to separate language into those parts which have purely objective significance, and those parts which are 'subjective'. However, so far in modern philosophy, drawing such a line has proved to be impossible to achieve in an agreed manner, not least because language itself is required to draw the line. If language resists a definitive separation between the subjective and the objective, the kind of philosophy which tries to show how the subjective mind more or less successfully mirrors or represents the nature of the objective world can be questioned. Claims about objectivity depend on the use of language, and language itself cannot be said to be either purely objective or purely subjective.

Despite frequent claims to the contrary, the everyday sense of truth need not be deeply affected by such ideas. Sceptics cannot make contentions about language's incapacity to express truth without presupposing that the truth of their own claims could be conveyed by language. The new ideas about language instead pose questions about what it means to express the truth. Saying that something is purely objective would require a meta-perspective, outside of language – the 'view from nowhere' – and the idea is that this is put in question by the need to characterize that perspective in language itself. Truth may therefore be a notional goal which motivates inquiry, rather than something that we ever definitively know we have grasped. Twentieth-century philosophy will involve instructive conflicts between approaches that seek to restrict the scope of the truth to verifiable statements, as a means of trying to ensure complete objectivity, and approaches that extend the scope of truth to any articulation which makes manifest an aspect of the world. In the latter approach, art can be a vehicle of truth, when it reveals or makes new sense of a perspective on the world. The latter approaches inherit much from what is initiated by Hamann and Herder.

While one can ignore many of the historical and stylistic issues in Kant's texts and still use them in contemporary philosophy, the complex, allusive style of Hamann's texts cannot be separated from their content. His texts create a web of associations that connect aspects of the world in often unexpected ways. Language, for Hamann, is not best seen in terms of defining the meanings of words. It is instead a celebration of the diversity of divine creation, which opens up ever new perspectives. There is an endless process of translation 'from a language of angels into a human language, that is, thoughts into words, – things into names, – images into signs'. The 'literary' aspect of language is, then, not a contingent addition to language, but its core. When Hamann criticizes Kant, for example, he does so in a highly rhetorical manner. Before we get to the Kantian question of how objective knowledge is possible, Hamann contends:

> another main question remains: *how the capacity of thinking is possible?* – The capacity to think *right* and *left*, *before* and *without*, *with* and *beyond* experience? One needs no deduction to prove the genealogical priority of *language* before the *seven* holy functions of logical propositions and conclusions and their heraldry.

What this baroque passage means becomes apparent in relation to Hamann's concern with the dangers of abstraction.

A great deal of modern philosophy since Descartes has been concerned with a particular version of scepticism. Descartes separates mind and body by his claim that the only cognitive certainty is the mind's awareness of itself. Knowledge of the world of objects, including one's own body, is inherently open to doubt. Hamann does not accept the Cartesian picture, because it assumes that knowledge of the world based on rational justification is the essential basis of philosophy. He thinks instead that '*belief* happens as little in terms of reasons as *tasting* and *smelling*': our essential contact with the world is 'sensuous'. This contact is not to be understood in the terms of the 'empiricism' of Locke and others (who did, though, influence him), where 'sense data' are the sole source of knowledge. Hamann's concern is rather with how it is that we arrive at a world that is intelligible. Starting with a critical account of 'reason', in the manner of Kant's philosophy, does not explain how it is that there is reason at all, which has to do with the question of the origin of language.

Both Hamann and Herder seek to answer the question of why we need reason to understand language, but also need language to have reason, though neither of them really answers the question in a convincing manner. Hamann tries to use his idiosyncratic theology as a way out of the philosophical problem, by seeing, following the Jewish tradition of the Kabbalah, creation itself as a language, in which God's Word creates the thing it designates. His suspicion of abstraction derives from his idea that language originates from our practical, sensuous contact with the world. He consequently refuses to accept mathematics as the foundation of reason: instead, 'the only first and last organ and criterion of reason' is language, which is based on nothing more than tradition and use, and cannot be seen in terms of 'universal and necessary reliability'.

This stance will be vital to the emergence of the modern conception of 'hermeneutics', the art or science of interpretation. Hermeneutics is important for German philosophy's questioning of scientific accounts of language, and for its critique of 'scientism', the belief that the only warrantable truths are scientific ones. For hermeneutics, scientific questions cannot arise at all unless we already understand the world via our practical use of natural languages. The background pre-understandings involved in this cannot be explained by a scientific account, because the very intelligibility of that account would itself depend on them. The decisive idea, which, if correct, has devastating consequences for scientistic conceptions, is that understanding cannot be reduced to explanation, because explanation always presupposes some form of prior understanding.

Herder often does not share Hamann's theological concerns, but he is equally interested in the diversity of human languages. His distance from the idea that language simply represents things is very evident: 'Not how an expression can be etymologically derived and determined analytically, but how it is used is the question. Origin and use are often very different'. In his influential *Essay on the Origin of Language* of 1772, Herder fails to give a convincing answer to how we arrive at language without reason and reason without language, but he does suggest a key aspect of how we can differentiate the linguistic from the non-linguistic. Herder's idea is that we have the capacity for '*Besonnenheit*' ('reflection'), which enables one to pick out characteristics of things in the world, such as the bleating of a sheep. One can use an indefinite number of other terms to characterize a sheep, and it is precisely language's endless capacity to enable such discriminations that is its essential feature. Language makes us able to understand a sheep as a mammal, as lunch, as a symbol of Christ, as what produces certain countryside sounds, and so on. Herder's and Hamann's views are 'holistic': the world for them does not consist of a collection of particular nameable objects. Instead, what things are is determined by the ways in which other things are made manifest by language and other human activity. What a sheep is seen as depends on its place in a world of significances that emerge via the practices of a particular culture. The world therefore becomes a web of significances whose characteristics change as human relationships to the world change.

Schleiermacher

Herder's groundbreaking reflections on language are scattered all over his work, and are not notably consistent. It is Friedrich Daniel Ernst Schleiermacher (1768–1834) who develops the ideas outlined here into a more systematic and coherent conception. Many of Schleiermacher's insights have begun to re-emerge in the light of the failure of some of the analytical tradition to take sufficient account of the holistic nature of language. Schleiermacher has usually been presented as the theorist of 'empathetic' interpretation, in which one 'feels one's way' into the mind of an author. This view is simply false. Instead, his hermeneutics and other texts offer a sophisticated account of language, which depends on a version of philosophical ideas of the kind we will encounter in Chapter 3 (and he does not use the German word for 'empathy'). Schleiermacher confronts the tension between the view that meaning and language are controlled by intentions of the subject, and a view that language pre-exists the subject in the form of shared structures and rules.

Schleiermacher is best known as the theologian who was crucial to the development of modern Protestantism, and his theology gives a clue as to why language becomes so central to his thinking. Kant's demonstration that the main proofs of the existence of God are invalid meant that theology had to re-establish itself in a manner which does not rely on philosophical proof. Schleiermacher bases his theology on what he calls the 'feeling of absolute dependence' of the subject. He sees the subject, following Kant, as both receptive and spontaneous, but for him there is no fundamental difference between receptivity and spontaneity: both involve self and world in differing degrees. The sheer fact that we actively apprehend and interpret the world at all is, for Schleiermacher, inexplicable in philosophical terms. Although we can direct our mental and physical activity, we are not the source of our being active: this is given as part of our nature. We have to respond to this dependence in non-cognitive ways, because our knowledge depends on this activity too. The feeling that our activity connects to the activity of the rest of the living universe is what leads to religion. The sense of God is, then, based on this feeling of a connection to a greater whole which is not in our power.

Language too involves receptivity and spontaneity, and it entails another kind of dependence of the subject on something which it does not originate. The inherently social nature of language involves a sense of the dependence of the subject on the 'Other', but also a sense of human connectedness which takes the subject beyond itself. Schleiermacher's focus on language leads him in his texts on hermeneutics from 1805 onwards to influential reflections on problems of interpretation. He bases these on the tension between language as something pre-existing in society, and as something which individual subjects can use to express their individuality. The aim is to grasp the relationship between these two sides in the text or utterance to be interpreted. This task can never be definitively achieved, because one can never have access to all the contexts of an utterance, or all the motivations for it. Schleiermacher therefore makes it clear that interpretation is necessarily finite, and is a practice for which there can be no definitive rules.

This stance leads him to prescient ideas, which suggest why the approaches to language which were the initial basis for analytical philosophy are mistaken (see Chapter 7). Kant made a distinction between 'analytic' judgements that are true by virtue of the meanings of the words in them, such as 'A bachelor is an unmarried man', and 'synthetic' judgements, which require knowledge about the world, such as 'Fred Smith is a bachelor'. On the basis of this distinction, philosophers early in the 20th century, like Gottlob Frege and Bertrand Russell, seek to establish logical foundations for the understanding of language which are independent of contingent facts about the world derived from experience. Much subsequent effort has been devoted to trying to make this project work. In the 1950s, the American philosopher W. V. O. Quine argued that the distinction is untenable, because our understanding of any statement can be revised in the light of other true statements, there being no words which could be said to be definitively synonymous. This view echoes the holism we saw in Herder and Hamann, and, if accepted, spells the end of a project of philosophy based on the analysis of foundational concepts. The intriguing fact is that Schleiermacher made this point well before the idea of an 'analytical philosophy' even existed. In his posthumously published *Dialectic*, he says that:

> The difference between analytical and synthetic judgements is a fluid one, of which we take no account...This difference...just expresses a different state of the formation of concepts.

What counts as analytic will in other contexts not count as such, there being no stable foundational concepts outside of the changing web of language. Consideration of the history of German philosophy's approaches to language after Kant can suggest how much was ignored in the establishing of the Anglo-American analytical philosophy of language. The reason the German approaches were ignored has to do with the analytical desire for philosophy to compete in rigour with the natural sciences. Whether this is the best course for philosophy to take will be an issue in the coming chapters.

Chapter 3
German Idealism

What is German Idealism?

The modern subject can be interpreted as, in Kant's phrase, 'giving the law' both to nature (in the sciences) and to itself (in moral self-determination), and yet as being afflicted by a sense of 'homelessness', which results from its questioning of theology and of traditional roles and identities. Kant sought to sustain the idea of self-determination by locating freedom in a domain which was not subject to the laws of nature. At the same time, nature 'in itself' was inaccessible to human knowledge. How, then, does nature in itself relate to human freedom? 'German Idealism', which emerges in the 1790s, aims to rethink the relationship between the subjective and the objective in the light of Kant's claims. How does our 'spontaneous' power to 'give the law' to nature relate to the nature to which the law is given? This power must in one sense be given to us by nature itself, because we are natural beings. However, unlike the rest of nature, the power cannot appear, because it is precisely what makes it possible to think about nature objectively, 'as appearance', at all. That to which things appear cannot be a thing in the same way as what appears. This means that claims about our legislative power cannot be based on objective evidence about the mind, such as might be gained from a science of psychology, because that science itself also depends on that power. The idea which German Idealism sees as implicit in

Kant is, then, that knowledge, which depends on the spontaneity of judgement, and self-determined, spontaneous action, can be seen as sharing the same source, and this source is not accessible to the kind of investigation carried out in the sciences. This idea leads to two essential possibilities, which intersect at certain points.

One possibility sees 'subjectivity', the 'I' in the very broad sense it often has for German Idealism, as the basis of there being a 'world' at all, rather than an unarticulated chaos. 'Subjectivity' is therefore what generates durable forms, via which nature becomes something living and intelligible. Without the 'light' shone by thinking on nature, nature would be opaque to itself. This kind of approach can be made sense of by the thought that the matter of which organisms consist is replaced during their life, without them becoming something different. The idea is that this suggests the primacy of a certain kind of conception of 'mind', in the sense of that which gives rise to intelligible forms, over nature: without the activity of mind, nothing determinate can emerge at all. The core of philosophy thus becomes the activity of the subject, not the explanation of the objective natural world.

The other possibility is that both the activity of the mind and freedom are inherent in nature's own 'productivity'. Nature is again not simply an objective system of laws, because it 'produces' subjectivity, by which it comes to knowledge of itself and becomes capable of self-determination, rather than remaining enclosed within itself. Nature's productivity is, though, not ultimately in our control: even our thinking 'happens', it is not something we consciously make ourselves do. Once thought emerges, there is a degree of self-determination in thought: the question is how decisive this self-determination actually is. The thinking subject is here not fully transparent to itself and depends to some degree on something 'unconscious'.

Both these alternatives share the idea that, although changes in nature are determined by laws, the very fact that nature is structured at all, and is dynamic rather than static, is not determined in the same way. Ideas relating to the first of these alternatives are associated with Salomon Maimon (1754–1800) and Johann Gottlieb Fichte (1762–1814), the second with the 'nature philosophy' of Friedrich Wilhelm Joseph Schelling (1775–1854). Georg Wilhelm Friedrich Hegel (1770–1831) tries to get beyond the differences between these alternatives by, as we shall

2. F. W. J. Schelling, 1848

see, describing the relationship between subjective and objective in a new way. From the end of the 1820s onwards, Schelling will argue that Hegel's version of Idealism cannot grasp central features of human existence.

In modernity, the sense of belonging to a meaningful whole becomes hard to sustain, and urbanization means that direct contact with nature tends to diminish for large parts of the population. Nature is also increasingly subordinated to the effects of science's analysis of its elements. This subordination gives priority to objectifying approaches over other ways of making sense of the world. The consequence can be a repression of certain aspects of ourselves, such as the need to experience the world as intrinsically meaningful: the sociologist Max Weber will later term this emptying of meaning from nature the 'disenchantment' of the world. However, there are probably, as the ecological crisis now shows, limits to humankind's ability to subject nature to itself. Schelling already makes critical remarks about the damaging effects of regarding nature as just the object of human goals at the end of the 18th century. Similarly, a brief manifesto, often referred to as the 'Oldest System-Programme of German Idealism', of 1796 (whose author is Schelling, Hegel, or their friend, the poet Friedrich Hölderlin, 1770–1843), demands a 'mythology of reason'. This would harmonize the new scientific worldview with the symbolic forms employed in people's everyday lives. What modern science tells us is to be reconciled with decisions on what should be done by finding ways of communicating and evaluating knowledge that engage the aesthetic and moral imagination of all levels of society, in the way that mythology supposedly did in traditional societies. Although this vision will come to be seen as unrealizable, the contradictions that occasioned it are still apparent in the failure of humankind's ever increasing technological capacity to bring about a more just and humane world.

German Idealism also tries to resolve contradictions which result from the erosion of the order exemplified by the idea that the king's authority derives from God. The beheading of the king in both the English and the French revolutions epitomizes changes in the nature of legitimacy characteristic of modernity. Order now has to be freely established by human beings, without appeals to a higher authority. Human interests are, though, inherently divergent, especially when social mobility increases as a result of the rise of capitalism, so how can authority be universally legitimated? The French Revolution implements the Terror in the name of Reason, and the ways in which universal principles can lead to inhumanity suggest the need for new approaches to the reconciliation of individual and society. The difficulties this reconciliation involves are apparent in the fact that Hegel's work on this issue in the *Philosophy of Right* (1820) has been read as a proto-totalitarian defence of the power of the state which stands above the individual. Things are, though, not so simple: as Hegel argues, without a law-governed social order, the individual would have no rights anyway. Rights depend upon acknowledgement that the law applies both to oneself and to others. Understanding the interdependence of opposed terms, like that between the 'general will' of the state and the will of the individual, lies at the heart of German Idealist thinking, which seeks to overcome the contradictions, both social and philosophical, that arise from the end of feudalism.

Sources of German Idealism

German Idealism is not an idealism like Berkeley's, in which 'being is perceiving'. However, one of its sources is the question of whether Kant is, despite himself, a Berkeleyan idealist. Kant rejects idealism: even though we only know things via the way we perceive them, they still exist 'in themselves'. How, though, do appearances relate to things in themselves? In 1789, Friedrich Heinrich Jacobi (1743–1819) questions Kant's claim that things in themselves *cause* appearances. For Kant, a cause links one appearance to another that necessarily succeeds it. Things in themselves do not appear, so they cannot, in Kant's own terms, be said to cause appearances. This seems to leave an alternative between either getting rid of things in themselves altogether, by adopting full-scale idealism, or abandoning transcendental idealism, at the risk of going back to the kind of 'dogmatic' metaphysics Kant had criticized. Negotiating what is at issue in this alternative constitutes a core task for German Idealism.

Jacobi's questions about the direction of philosophy at this time make it clear why the concerns of the German Idealists are more than abstractly epistemological. The so-called 'Pantheism Controversy', which began in 1783, arose over Jacobi's claim that the Enlightenment writer G. E. Lessing had admitted to being a Spinozist. Spinoza had been excommunicated from the Dutch Jewish church for atheism in 1656, and atheism was still unacceptable to the ruling powers in 18th-century Germany. At the end of the century, Fichte loses his academic job because he is seen as an atheist. Spinoza's God is not the creator and legislator of the world, but rather the organized totality of nature: God and nature are the same. In Spinoza's system, what things are depends on their not being other things, rather than on anything intrinsic to themselves. Each particular thing 'conditions' other things, and they in turn condition it. Jacobi argues that this leads to a regress of 'conditions of conditions', in which no explanation can be definitively justified. Grounding knowledge therefore requires something 'unconditioned'. For Jacobi, this is God, who makes particulars meaningful parts of a world that we invest in cognitively, morally, and emotionally, rather than just parts of a mechanical system. The regress of explanations is stopped in Jacobi's view by the realization that our 'faith/belief' [*Glaube*] in reality cannot be justified in cognitive terms (which lead to the regress just described), and so has to have recourse to theology. However, if the unconditioned is to serve as a *philosophical* explanation (i.e. one that does not see God as the explanation of the world of conditions), one ends up in the contradictory situation of 'having to discover *conditions* of the *unconditioned*', because explanation is, precisely, finding the conditions of something.

German Idealism therefore tries to find new ways of explicating the 'unconditioned' or the 'Absolute'. In modern science, things are explained by seeking conditions of conditions. Jacobi's concern is that this means that there is no ultimate legitimation for science: one can always seek more causal explanations, but there can be no ultimate reason for doing so. Moreover, science can only function in a world which has already revealed itself as intelligible *before* we seek scientific accounts of it. (This point will later form the core of Heidegger's thinking.) Jacobi regards what ensues from Spinozism as 'nihilism', because it offers no account of how it is that being is intelligible at all. The reason for engaging in scientific activity must be located in the sphere of human action, but how action can be legitimated is the problem to which understanding the Absolute would be the solution.

German Idealism can therefore be understood as exploring the idea that subjectivity is 'unconditioned'. In his attempts around 1789–90 to make Kant more convincing to a wider audience, Karl Leonhard Reinhold insisted that thought needed a foundation if a regress of the kind Jacobi described was to be avoided. He argued that the 'fact of consciousness' was not itself conditioned, because it is what enables us to be aware of conditions at all. Maimon contended that Kant's division between the receptive and the spontaneous could not be sustained. The existence of the objective world is inferred from the supposed causality of things in themselves, but the category of causality depends on the subject, not on the object, and what is caused are perceptions of the *subject*. The subject–object relationship therefore just entails two kinds of consciousness, rather than subjective consciousness and a separate objective world. The world appears to be objective because what produces perceptions of the 'external world' is the 'unconscious' side of the subject. Hamann's idea that the receptive and the spontaneous cannot be wholly separate is crucial for German Idealism. If apparently passive receptivity and active spontaneity are in fact different degrees of the same 'activity', the gap between subject and world can be closed. Consciousness would then be seen as 'of the world' in two senses: it belongs to the world, as something which emerges from nature, and it makes the world into the object of knowledge and action. The question is how to interpret these two senses.

Fichte

Fichte's central assumption is that the self-determining activity of the subject is the core of philosophy. The subject can apprehend the world in objective terms, but cannot itself be wholly objectified. For Fichte, the self-determining subject must not be conditioned by anything external to it: if it were explicable via what conditions it, it would be just an object determined by natural laws. Human subjects could conceivably just be very complex robots: for Fichte, though, it is the ability of subjects to 'reflect' which means that this cannot be the case. What makes it possible for us to reflect on our knowledge and action is not a cause of the kind that we encounter in nature, but rather our freedom. The 'I' that can reflect therefore involves something 'absolute', not conditioned by anything outside itself. In reflection, the subjective makes part of *itself* into something objective, but it is not caused to do this by something objective. The situation of deciding to be critical of oneself can suggest what is meant here: by doing so, one 'inhibits' oneself in order to appreciate the objective significance of what one has done. In Fichte's terms, the basic process is seen as the 'absolute I', which involves nothing that depends on anything else, splitting itself and so establishing the relationship between subjective and objective, I and not-I.

Because one can see the universe itself in analogous terms – the universe becomes an object separate from the subject when consciousness arises – it is not always clear how Fichte intends his conception. Before consciousness exists, the universe is 'in itself', afterwards it becomes 'for itself' – terms that Jean-Paul Sartre, for example, will later use in relation to the individual subject. '*Gegenstand*' – 'object' – means that which 'stands against' something else, in this case the I. For Fichte, the 'absolute I' splits into a relative subject and object, but the subjective must keep overcoming the objective, otherwise the world would never develop. The objective universe can only be experienced *as* objective by a subject, so the latter must be prior. The point of existence is, then, to be found in the activity of the subject, in practical rather than theoretical reason.

Commentators on Fichte are still not agreed on precisely what he means: how, for example, do individual human subjects, who may in fact rarely exercise their freedom, relate to the generative principle of subjectivity involved in the 'absolute I'? Fichte describes the 'I' as a 'deed-action', a '*Tathandlung*', as opposed to a '*Tatsache*', a 'fact'. The 'I' is an absolute beginning because it derives from nothing but itself: otherwise self-determination is an illusion. However, in his claim that '*the consciousness of a thing outside us is absolutely nothing else than the product of our own capacity for thinking*', only the *consciousness* of the thing outside us is the product of the capacity for thinking, not the thing itself, so he could be seen as offering a version of Kant's transcendental idealism. But how is one to grasp the 'I' in philosophy without turning it into an object? Fichte's answer is that this takes place via 'intellectual intuition', 'that through which I know something because I do it', rather than knowing it as something objective. Much of German Idealism's subsequent development revolves around the implications of this term.

The reason is that intellectual intuition has to do with how philosophy characterizes mind's connection to the world. Kant had seen intellectual intuition as the kind of thought characteristic of the deity, which creates the real object by thinking it. This meant that he denied the possibility of such intuition for finite intellects like ours. For Fichte, it is the coincidence in intellectual intuition of the act of thinking with what is thought that overcomes the idea of a gap between mind and world. But isn't this, as Jacobi will object, a kind of narcissism, in which thinking just mirrors itself to itself? The weight Fichte places on the subject seems to leave no space for any independence of the world of nature, which becomes merely the object of human activity. Moreover, the justification of the emphasis on the 'I' depends on the act of intellectual intuition, which can only be accessible via the act of reflecting. How does one subject's reflection relate to another subject's reflection? Fichte's emphasis on individual self-determination echoes vital social and political changes in the modern world, but it also suggests dangers. From Schelling to Heidegger and beyond, the problems of the modern world are often seen as relating to the subject's drive to dominate what is opposed to it.

Schelling

After initially proposing a position close to Fichte's, Schelling comes to accuse Fichte of reducing nature to being the object of human purposes, when it should also be understood as a source of meaning and purpose. At the end of the 18th century, the development of a new appreciation of the beauty and grandeur of non-human nature is linked to the search for orientation in a world which is increasingly regarded as lacking theological foundations. The emergence of the discipline of aesthetics in Kant's third Critique was also closely connected to a revaluation of humankind's relationships to nature. It is no coincidence, then, that Schelling's early work both tries to develop a new conception of nature, and sees art as a way of understanding the relationship between mind and world.

Schelling's 'philosophy of nature' ('*Naturphilosophie*') can best be approached via the notion of 'self-organization'. When an organism develops by the interaction of its constituents it becomes more than the sum of its law-bound material parts. Schelling sees organic development as connected to human self-determination, because both involve more than determination by natural laws. The need to connect ourselves to nature more adequately is apparent in the Cartesian split between mind and nature: 'one can push as many transitory materials as one wants... between mind and matter, but sometime the point must come where mind and matter are One'. Schelling takes up Spinoza's distinction between *natura naturans*, nature which is 'productive', and *natura naturata*, the objective 'products' of nature. The former suggests an alternative conception of nature to that present in the natural sciences. The vital fact about nature here is that it involves life and develops into new forms. Whereas the sciences rely on analysis of the parts, nature philosophy is concerned with the organic connections between those parts. In the light of the ecological crisis, such an approach seems prescient: it suggests how piecemeal analysis by particular sciences may be unable to grasp the interaction of separate, but ultimately connected, aspects of nature as a whole. Schelling's philosophy of nature aims to connect nature's 'unconscious productivity' with mind's 'conscious productivity'. Thought is where 'nature first completely returns into itself', and it reveals that 'nature is originally identical with what is known in us as intelligent and conscious'. Without thought, nature is opaque; without nature, thought could not occur at all. The task is therefore to understand the move from unconscious to conscious productivity.

A division emerges here in German philosophy, between theories that seek a complete conceptual account of how mind and world relate, and approaches that appeal to non-conceptual forms of 'intuition'. The danger of the latter is that they can lead to a neglect of rational argument. However, there are serious grounds for certain kinds of appeal to 'intuition'. In his *System of Transcendental Idealism* (1800), Schelling contends that works of art are the objective manifestation of 'intellectual intuition'. If intellectual intuition is located within the subject, as Fichte's knowing by doing is, it is unclear how it can play a justificatory role in philosophy. For Schelling, the production of art requires unconscious productivity, which takes the artist beyond what is governed by the existing rules of an artistic medium. By manifesting this unconscious productivity in something objective that can be consciously apprehended, art shows what philosophy cannot say. Art is therefore the 'organ of philosophy', a publicly accessible medium which expresses how conscious and unconscious are connected. If we regard a work of art as an object of knowledge to be determined by concepts, we will not grasp how it can change the subject's relationship to the world. Art can do this because it can always be interpreted in new ways. This makes art's meaning in one sense 'indeterminate', because it cannot be definitively established. Rather than being a philosophical failing, however, this indeterminacy, which makes the work in one sense 'infinite', shows how the world of finite knowledge might be transcended, without making 'dogmatic' philosophical claims.

Schelling does not sustain the idea of art as the reconciliation of subjective and objective. He comes to think that if there were a harmony between subjective and objective, freedom would be just part of the overall purpose of nature, and everything would be decided in advance. From around 1809 onwards, Schelling therefore radicalizes the idea of freedom by seeing it in terms of the possibility of doing evil by asserting one's will in a manner not governed by existing norms. Without this possibility, the 'essence' of freedom, which requires a sense of contingent open-endedness, is lacking. Schelling does not deny the necessities in rational thought or stop trying to develop a systematic philosophy. He does, though, question the idea that reason can account for its own existence, and so introduces a fundamental contingency into thinking which is at odds with the Idealist project of reconciling mind and world.

The task of Schelling's later philosophy becomes to understand how an intelligible world emerges at all from a pre-rational state. From around the end of the 1820s until his death in 1854, he questions the very possibility of realizing the aims of German Idealism:

> Far...from man and his activity making the world comprehensible, he is himself what is most incomprehensible, and continually drives me to the opinion of the unhappiness of all being...Precisely he, man, drives me to the last despairing question: why is there anything at all? why is there not nothing?

He thinks that Hegel's attempt to answer the problems of modern philosophy in terms of how 'man and his activity make the world comprehensible' fails to confront the dissonance between thought and being that goes to the heart of our attempts to understand ourselves. This sense of dissonance leads Schelling to new

3. G. W. F. Hegel

reflections on how philosophy relates to pre-philosophical forms of mythological thinking, and on philosophy's relation to religion.

Hegel

Hegel is notorious for such claims as 'the real is the rational', which seem to suggest that there is no philosophical basis for questioning to what extent the world is rationally constituted, and are strikingly at odds with the assertions just cited from Schelling. These claims led Karl Marx and others to see Hegel as a defender of an unjust political status quo in a still feudal Germany. Schelling and Hegel were friends until they fell out around the time of the publication of Hegel's *Phenomenology of Mind/Spirit* (hereafter *PM*) (the German word '*Geist*' can be translated either way, depending on the context) in 1807. How did they come to the divergence in their assessments of the capacity for philosophy to comprehend the modern world? One way to answer this is via the question of 'intuition' and its relationship to scepticism. As modern science establishes itself, it becomes apparent that very many firmly held traditional beliefs are untenable. But what is to say that the new scientific beliefs are not equally open to doubt, especially as modern science lives from refuting theories and replacing them with better ones? The appeal to intellectual intuition is intended to establish a fundamental contact between thought and reality that would obviate scepticism, but Fichte and Schelling share the problem that the notion of intuition cannot, by definition, be articulated in concepts. It is either something that only free individuals are capable of (Fichte), or something that we understand via art's showing how subjective and objective are connected (early Schelling).

Hegel argues that intellectual intuition cannot be presupposed at the beginning of a philosophical system, as the basis on which the rest is built. It can only be arrived at after philosophy has gone through and articulated the ways in which thought and the real interact. These can range from primitive reactions of organisms to their environment to the highest forms of conceptual thinking, in which philosophy reflects on how it itself became possible. Whether this is an adequate response to what is involved in the issue of intuition is crucial to assessing Hegel's philosophy.

For Hegel, an understanding of *why* particular truth claims turn out to be false turns the sceptical position against itself. This is because knowledge can never begin from something 'immediate', in the sense of something which does not need to relate to anything else to be what it is. Accounts of the solar system, for example, do not begin with 'immediate' data that are then explained in a theory. They begin rather with an already 'mediated' mythological interpretation of the nature of the heavenly bodies. This interpretation is made more systematic in Ptolemaic astronomy, and then is changed again when Copernicus and Galileo demonstrate the heliocentric nature of the solar system. The more plausible theory results from the revelation of the faults in the preceding theory, not from immediate access to the truth.

Hegel terms this process 'determinate negation': refuted theories are not just thrown away, they make possible better theories. Philosophy shows how each particular understanding of something involves an inadequacy that leads to a more complete account. Eventually, the demonstration of such inadequacies leads to the articulation in a philosophical system of all the ways things can relate to each other. This system culminates in the 'absolute idea', the explanation of why all particular truths depend on their relationships to other truths for their justification. There are, therefore, no definitive positive claims until the deficiencies have been shown in all particular claims.

The *PM* traces the structures involved in how mind 'appears'. The idea that mind appears, rather than being that to which the world appears, indicates the nature of the approach. Looking at how the subject can be in true contact with the object may be the wrong way to consider the theory of knowledge. Hegel uses the metaphor of learning to swim. Unless one goes in the water, one cannot learn to swim, in the same way as one cannot know without always already being involved with what is to be known. The *PM* gives a genetic account of the historical relationships between subject and object, which Kant saw in terms of timeless categories of thought. For thought to develop at all, something has to be lacking. Even at the instinctual level, the core relationship of something lacking an 'other' is present. Living beings need food and they need to propagate: without the 'other' they cannot exist. Everything is therefore in some respect both itself and not itself: the food you eat is not you, but it becomes you. The overcoming of a lack means that the subject depends on the object, but this dependence is not in itself the basis of further development. It is only when a sustained awareness of the dependence develops that thought emerges, in the form, for example, of the memory of what fulfils a need.

Terry Pinkard has referred to Hegel's conception as an account of the 'sociality of reason'. The *PM* explains how dependence makes possible new kinds of relationships between people and things. From the situation where the self always sees the other as a threat – Hegel is thinking of Hobbes's 'war of all against all' that precedes legal relations – emerges the ability to grant that the other has rights in the same way as I do. Indeed, without mutual acknowledgement between self and other, rights have no concrete form of existence at all. In a famous passage of the *PM*, on 'Lordship and Bondage', the lord consumes the products of the bondsman whom he has subordinated to himself. The lord's resulting dependence on the bondsman enables the latter to develop his own capacity to manipulate the world, to the point where he can become more powerful than the lord. The passage is both a model of how intersubjective power-relations change people and their relationship to the world, and a historical reflection on how this model is manifest in the demise of the feudal aristocracy in the French Revolution.

This combination of theoretical abstraction and concrete reference to history illustrates Hegel's idea that philosophy is 'its age written in thought', rather than a timeless true representation of the world. There are, however, conflicting impulses in Hegel, between a) the idea that thought is generated by particular historical interactions between people and their world, which is one way of reading the *PM*, and b) the aim of giving a definitive philosophical account of the structures of all such interactions, which is what he offers in the *Science of Logic* (1812–16). The former may point to the 'end of philosophy', because it no longer requires an account of the ultimate nature of things. The latter insists that a historicized account of truth must itself be true in a way which is not subject to historical change. Different interpretations of Hegel depend on which aspect is seen as essential in his philosophy.

Hegel is often seen as a very speculative thinker, which led him to be ignored in most Anglo-American analytical philosophy until recently. However, the issue of 'immediacy' suggests a different picture. Many analytical philosophers have regarded 'sense data' as the basis of knowledge, because observational evidence is essential to good science. This philosophical view of sense data is, though, precisely an example of 'immediacy'. In the *PM*, Hegel takes the apparently most obvious 'immediate' certainty of the data in front of oneself in the present. This takes the form of (in my case) this computer, here, now. However, because particular perceptions must always be mediated by the general concepts we use to identify them, there is nothing intelligible in unconceptualized data at all. Hegel points out that the 'indexical' terms – 'this', 'here', and 'now' – are universals, which already mediate the content of my perception by enabling me to focus on something particular. Here becomes this window if I look out of it now, instead of writing. This claim involves a variant of the basic structure of Hegelian thought. Each this, here, and now negates the preceding and the succeeding this, here, and now, so all lack something, but the totality of thises, heres, and nows is the positive totality of space and time. The truth of the particular emerges through its mediation by general concepts, otherwise it is indeterminate. As in Kant, if there were no intuitions, concepts would be empty, and without concepts intuitions would be blind.

Hegel's 'dialectic' is the process in which the material and the form of our relationships to the world change in relation to each other. For Hegel, the 'concept' of an object is not just (as it is for Kant) a rule for identifying something, but instead includes all the ways in which the thing is grasped by our engaging with it. There is consequently no 'thing in itself', because the thing only becomes a something by being for us. Kant's 'thing in itself', Hegel maintains, is the result of abstracting from the thing everything that we know about it. This leaves us with no real thing at all, merely an indeterminate general notion. The thing's apparent immediacy is actually arrived at by mediation, the negation of what we already know of it.

These patterns of thought are used by Hegel to characterize all the main dimensions of the modern world, from science, to law and politics, to history, and to art. The move from indeterminate immediacy to mediation depends on relating things more and more extensively to what they are not. In the *Philosophy of Right*, for example, the 'immediate' individual gains their initial identity through the family, but the demands of the family are particular and require the law of the state if they are to be reconciled with the demands of other families. The problem here is, though, that the legitimacy present for Hegel in the higher level can, in concrete situations, lead to a repression of the supposedly lower level.

Hegel's criticisms of a reliance on immediacy are often plausible, and they play a role in contemporary challenges to the assumptions of much Anglo-American analytical philosophy. Why, though, was there a reaction against Hegel from the 1830s onwards, and again in analytical philosophy from early in the

20th century until very recently? One reason for the reaction in the 1830s is the clash of Hegel's claims concerning the power of reason with the sense that the rational capacities which bring about the major changes in 19th-century society can lead to irrational forms of social organization. Sending children down mines hardly confirms the rationality of the real. Later the rhetoric of Hegel's work, which deals in such terms as 'world spirit', would come into conflict with the growing attention to empirical detail in the natural sciences, which are the point of orientation of analytical philosophy.

It is, though, often ignored that in 'early German Romanticism', which begins in the mid-1790s, an alternative approach to that of Hegel already emerges, which shares some ideas with Hegel, but parts company with core elements of German Idealism. A Hegelian stance can point to how rationality does seem to make irrevocable advances, of the kind present in the realizations that, for example, slavery is indefensible and that women should not be treated as inferior to men. A Romantic stance would not necessarily deny that such realizations are irrevocable, but would question the kind of big philosophical story a Hegelian uses to explain why they are, on the grounds that a unitary story of the advance of Reason may obscure other resources for the generation of meaning in the modern world.

Chapter 4
'Early Romantic' philosophy

Irony

It might seem obvious that philosophy's goal is to find out the definitive truth about the world. Friedrich Schlegel (1772–1829), who, with Novalis (Georg Philipp Friedrich von Hardenberg) (1772–1801), is the most significant member of the group usually referred to as the 'early German Romantics', suggests, however, that this goal might not be quite so obvious: 'In truth you would be distressed if the whole world, as you demand, were for once seriously to become completely comprehensible'. A key aspect of early German Romantic philosophy, which is the product of a brief period at the end of the 18th century in Jena, is that it asks radical questions about the primary task of philosophy. If we think of philosophy from the vantage point of epistemology, the task is to find out how to arrive at knowledge. Whether a definitive answer to scepticism would make any real difference to most people's relationship to the world is, though, open to doubt. Overcoming scepticism was seen by Hegel as depending on what gives rise to scepticism: the fact that truths are constantly being negated. His approach no longer concentrates on whether our thinking fails to be in touch with 'reality', because 'reality' *is* precisely the process of negation occasioned by the interaction of subject and object, which cannot be described from an extra-mundane viewpoint. The 'view from nowhere' involves, for Hegel, the same problem as

Kant's 'thing in itself': it requires the abstraction of taking away everything that we know of the object.

In a lecture of 1801, Schlegel already suggests the idea which points in the direction of what Hegel will call 'determinate negation': 'Truth arises when opposed errors neutralize each other'. Schlegel's approach is 'ironic': for him, positive assertions of truth are always likely to be revoked, in the way that an ironic statement revokes its literal meaning. Hegel's response to this kind of irony is to look for where the negative becomes the positive; Romantic philosophy, in contrast, thinks that there may be no final end to irony. This might seem to lead to the problem that claims about the relativity of all truth must themselves be absolute. Schlegel, though, is aware of this objection: 'If all truth is relative, then the proposition is also relative that all truth is relative'. So how does one sustain a sense of the Absolute which would enable one to avoid this paradox?

The problem revealed by the Romantic view is that knowing one has reached the final truth would entail a prior familiarity with that truth, otherwise it would be impossible to recognize that it is the final truth. This familiarity would have to be something like Fichte's intellectual intuition, which the Romantics already questioned from the mid-1790s onwards. Novalis says, 'We everywhere seek the unconditioned [*das Unbedingte*], and always only find things [*Dinge*]'. Dissatisfaction with the limitations of finite knowledge leads to a sense of the infinite, rather than there being a founding positive knowledge of the essential nature of the infinite. The dissatisfaction cannot, however, be removed by gaining philosophical access to the infinite. For Novalis, the 'Absolute which is given to us can only be known negatively, by our acting and finding that no action can reach what we are seeking'. What philosophy has sought is an absolute 'basis' (*Grund*) that would allow it to complete itself. However, 'If this were not given, if this concept contained an impossibility – then the drive to philosophize would be an endless activity'. Philosophy itself therefore takes on a different status, coming closer to what is present in the modern experience of art, where there are no definitive interpretations, only new perspectives.

Mediation and 'longing'

Hegel and the early Romantics share ideas concerning the modern situation, in which many truths seem inherently transient. However, their differences suggest a paradigmatic division in modern philosophy. This is between positions in which the subject overcomes the contradictory nature of modern reality in philosophy, and positions which suspect that by doing this the subject will find in the world only that which mirrors itself back to it. The aim of making thought wholly transparent to itself that is the basis of German Idealism's conception of self-determination may, then, turn out to be an illusion. Jacobi and Schleiermacher already objected to Fichte on this basis. In 1799, Jacobi argues against Fichte that 'The root of reason [*Vernunft*] is listening [*Vernehmen*]. – Pure reason is a listening which only listens to itself'. Hegel claims that his system is definitive, such that reason, by reflecting on its relations to the world, becomes transparent to itself. Here too reason is in danger of listening only to itself.

The power of Hegel's claims lies, as recent commentators have stressed, in the fact that denying them involves an appeal to something immediate. Nietzsche will claim that the real motivation of thought is the unconscious drives of the subject, rather than the pure search for the truth. This claim must, though, itself be justified, and justification requires mediation. How do we *know* that thought is based on the unconscious? If we cite evidence such as Freudian slips, via which we infer that the source of a person's utterance or action is not the one they think it is, we are already involved in mediation. This brings the issue into what is now called the 'space of reasons', by explaining the mechanism of repression that leads to the slips. The Hegelian position here relates to his arguments about sense-certainty. All forms of supposedly immediate evidence must be questioned via shared cognitive norms. Any attempt to circumvent such norms requires a legitimation that involves an appeal to other norms, which themselves require legitimation.

Hegel's approach seems very plausible, although the fact that social norms are always highly contested suggests an obvious difficulty. This difficulty does not mean, however, that there is another way of justifying something. The Romantic approach, on the other hand, is concerned that systematic philosophical completeness, of the kind they see in Fichte, may exclude much that is essential to our relationship to the world. Schlegel and Novalis do not deny the need for systematic coherence, but they see it in terms of 'systemlessness brought into a system'. Consider Novalis's remark that 'All the superstition and error of all times and peoples and individuals rests upon the confusion of the *symbol* with what is symbolized – upon making them identical – upon the belief in true complete representation'. The attraction of the Hegelian position with respect to scepticism lies in how it obviates the need for a founding argument which says how mind and world relate. Hegel does, however, aim at making the symbol (the system) and what is symbolized (being, the world) identical. If one accepts that in cognitive matters there can be no appeal to foundational evidence, a Hegelian position offers a convincing alternative. Anything which claims to be true must be subject to mediation, and, even if Hegel himself doesn't actually succeed, it seems possible that a systematic philosophical account of the dynamic structures of mediation could be achieved.

Perhaps the key question that emerges from Romantic philosophy, even before Hegel develops his system, is why such an account of the structures of rationality, which should reconcile us to the necessity of contradiction and suffering, might not overcome the modern sense of 'homelessness'. Schlegel maintains that 'If truth were found then the business of spirit would be completed and it would have to cease to be, since it only exists in activity'. Given that Schlegel has no faith that such a point could be reached, the core human experience is what he terms 'longing', his term for an inherent dissonance between ourselves and the world. Longing gives rise both to the desire to know, and to the feeling that knowledge does not always help to deal with the divided nature of existence. For that, we may need forms of expression which are not fully comprehensible in terms of knowledge. Think of how knowledge of the nature and the source of a psychological problem may not be enough to overcome the problem. Overcoming the problem may demand expressive activity that changes its very nature. The growing importance of music for philosophy at this time in Germany is a sign of what is at issue here: what music can do is not reducible to what we know about what it does.

Romantic philosophy and art

In his *Aesthetics*, Hegel announces the 'end of art' as the medium in which the highest insights of modern humankind can be expressed. Clearly there can be no replacement in the modern world for the way in which Greek tragedy helped to constitute the community in Athens. In this respect, Hegel is right. The resources that determine the modern world are, above all, political and legal relations that regulate human action, and the capacity of science and technology to solve problems. However, Hegel's claim is that philosophy takes over from religion and art the role of articulating the highest insights. The sciences only produce particular truths, which need to be connected to each other in a philosophical system. Since Hegel's time, however, modern philosophy rarely plays a very significant role in the actual functioning of the sciences. Hegel's elevation of philosophy may therefore be seen as in fact pointing to the 'end of philosophy'. If philosophy does not fulfil the role of ultimate arbiter, then the factors which really determine the nature of the modern world may render philosophy superfluous. Heidegger will argue that the sciences are where metaphysics since the Greeks was leading (see Chapter 8), because the aim of metaphysics was to provide the true picture of the world. Heidegger therefore seeks a different role for philosophy, which he, like the Romantics, connects to art.

But does the importance of art for these thinkers still matter to philosophy today? The difficulty here is highlighted by the fact that modern art has continually questioned its own very existence, as the frequently encountered response to avant-garde art of 'That's not art' suggests. One way to approach these issues is by considering the form in which Romantic philosophy is sometimes presented. If the message of philosophy cannot be separated from its 'medium', philosophy cannot be regarded as wholly different to art, where form is intrinsic to meaning. Although Schlegel did produce sustained, relatively systematic philosophical texts, he, like Novalis, is best known for his writing in fragments. Fragments only are fragments, rather than unconnected pieces of material, if they are broken parts of a whole. The whole is, though, what is missed in 'longing', not something that is known to exist as the goal of philosophy. In Fragment 116 of the collection of fragments from the *Athenaeum* journal, which ran from 1798 to 1800, Schlegel talks about Romantic art as a reflection of the world which 'can continually potentialize this reflection and multiply it as if in an endless row of mirrors'. Romantic art reminds us that the world is always more than we can say about it, that being transcends consciousness:

> Other forms of literature [*Poesie*, which has the sense of creative art] are finished and can now be completely analysed. The Romantic form of literature is still in a process of becoming; indeed that is its real essence, that it can eternally only become, and never be finished. It cannot be exhausted by any theory.

Whereas the sciences may aim at definitive knowledge of things, 'literature' sees how connecting things to other things, often in unexpected ways, may produce insights denied to the sciences.

4. *Evening Landscape with Two Men*, c. 1830–5, by Caspar David Friedrich

A significant tension emerges here, between the idea that the goal is to control the world more effectively, and the fear that this may render the world increasingly meaningless. In the latter perspective, the philosophical task is to create more meaning, which should be done with whatever resources are available. Schlegel asserts that 'Philosophy must begin with infinitely many propositions, according to its genesis (not with One proposition)', and, in a proto-pragmatist vein, that 'There are no basic propositions [*Grundsätze*] which would universally be appropriate accompanists and leaders to the truth.' It is not that Schlegel and Novalis reject the findings of science: Novalis was involved in scientific research. What they offer is a warning, which now seems prescient, against regarding the sciences as the sole sources of validity in the modern world.

The work of the early Romantics expresses something of the repressed energy in German intellectual life around the time of the French Revolution, for which philosophical and aesthetic innovation took the place of political revolution. The immediate effects of their work were fairly negligible: they were seen by many, including Hegel, as lacking philosophical seriousness. What is interesting, therefore, is how their concern to live creatively with uncertainty and diversity prefigures aspects of deconstructive and pragmatist thinking which are playing a role in contemporary revaluations of philosophy. In the face of the bewildering changes characteristic of modernity, Romantic philosophy reflects upon what can happen if one no longer looks for definitive solutions. This is a stance which can be both melancholy and liberating, and it would be some time before such a stance was widely adopted again. The desire for definitive solutions, of the kind offered by dogmatic theology, has, as we know, hardly gone away.

Chapter 5
Marx

The 'end of philosophy'

In debates which form the context of the work of Karl Marx (1818–83), people begin to talk for the first time of the 'end of philosophy'. But what does that mean? One way of bringing philosophy to an end would be to solve its essential problems. Hegel tries to do this, by giving a systematic answer to how divisions between subject and object could be overcome. What role is there, though, for philosophy, if Hegel's account is definitive? Significantly, Hegel has been read both as the ultimate metaphysician, and, more recently, as someone who offers a way out of traditional metaphysics. He does the latter by presenting an alternative to a 'God's eye view', in the idea that reason is solely a product of social relations. Both versions of Hegel could in fact be construed as ending philosophy, either by getting the ultimate version of metaphysics right, or by showing that established metaphysics is based on a misapprehension of the nature of the mind–world relationship.

Another way of ending philosophy is to regard its 'end' as its aim, which might be achieved by bringing about what is sought in the idea of the 'good life'. Doing so could obviate the reasons for asking about the meaning of life that result from the weakening of theological convictions. The fulfilments of the good life would

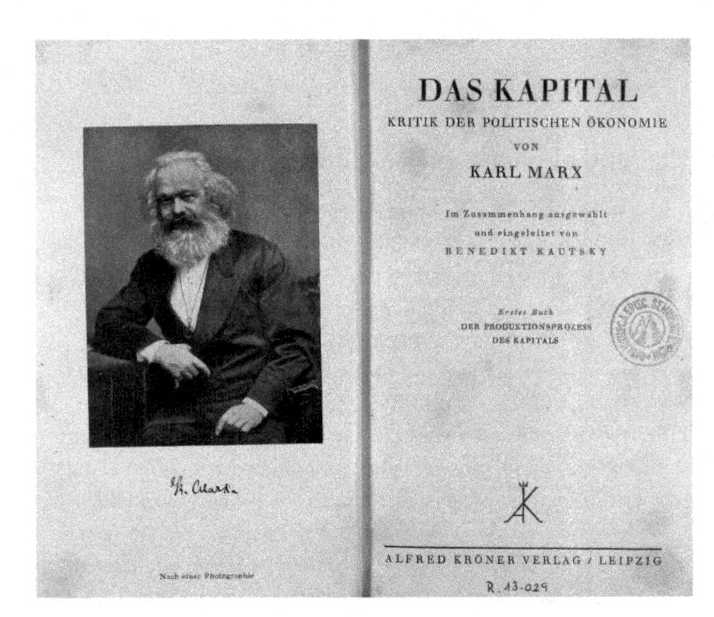

Nach einer Photographie

DAS KAPITAL

KRITIK DER POLITISCHEN ÖKONOMIE

VON

KARL MARX

Im Zusammenhang ausgewählt
und eingeleitet von
BENEDIKT KAUTSKY

Erstes Buch
DER PRODUKTIONSPROZESS
DES KAPITALS

ALFRED KRÖNER VERLAG / LEIPZIG

5. Karl Marx and *Das Kapital*

here make up for the pain that is inseparable from human life. From another angle: if one thinks, as both Marx and Nietzsche do, that metaphysics is in fact covert theology, an attack on theology will be an attack on philosophy. The target here is the idea of an account of the world that gets beyond a merely human perspective. A related 20th-century approach will be the attempt in analytical philosophy to show that many philosophical problems are 'pseudo-problems', occasioned by logical failures in the use of language. The way to end philosophy here is to show that it consists of questions which cannot have answers, because they are logically unsound.

Why, though, should versions of most of these ideas become a feature of 19th-century German philosophy, from the attacks on Hegel's philosophy of the 1830s onwards? Part of the answer is that philosophy now becomes very explicitly connected to politics. Kant, the Idealists, and the early Romantics were not apolitical: they all supported at least some aspects of the French Revolution and wrote on political philosophy. However, perhaps because of the repression to which radical political views were subjected by German states, they do not convey an explicit sense that political activity necessarily goes to the core of philosophy. One reason why a new kind of connection to politics becomes central is the awareness, initiated by Herder, Schlegel, and Hegel, that philosophy is subject to history in ways that had previously not been appreciated. The disruptive changes brought about by the scientific revolution, industrialization, and urbanization mean that the idea of a stable world order falls prey to the pressures of the historical world. Given the brutality that accompanies nascent capitalism, it is not surprising that suspicion of metaphysics becomes connected to the idea that philosophy may conspire with social injustice.

The 'Young Hegelians', a group of predominantly left-wing thinkers that included Ludwig Feuerbach (1804–72) and the early Marx, criticize Hegel but do not completely reject his ideas.

Their initial focus is religion, though their main objective is social transformation. One of the decisive changes in 19th-century theology is the incursion of new approaches to history into theology. This gives rise to questions about the historical basis of the Gospels, which is revealed to be very shaky. The wider truth of religion therefore becomes more questionable, and one response to this is the idea that the value of religion may not lie in the literal truth of the scriptures. The value of religion can be construed in both a destructive and a constructive manner. As a means of control that sustains traditional hierarchies, the value of religion for the ruling classes is as a form of 'ideology'. As a means of making life more tolerable when change seems impossible, religion keeps hope alive among the oppressed. Marx's remark about religion as the 'opium of the people' does not mean religion is something that just makes them sleep: it makes their pain tolerable. Without religion, though, many forms of authority lose their foundation, leaving the way open for radical social change. Such change needs, however, to offer in reality the kind of hope previously offered only to the imagination.

In Marx's period, there is a more and more explicit tension between an Enlightenment faith in reason's capacity for solving problems, and the tragic sense that human life is necessarily transient and painful. If there is no hope of individual redemption without religion, the hope has to be that the individual can contribute to the life of the species, by making a better future for humankind. However, whether the idea of such a future is a real consolation to the individual in distressing circumstances is by no means certain. Moreover, in the 19th century (and since), the individual goal of self-transcendence too often ends up taking the form of self-sacrifice to the political ends of the nation.

Feuerbach's strategy is to salvage the content of religion that is left when 'dogmatic' beliefs become untenable. He maintains, in a way later to be echoed by Freud, that the content of the notion of God is a 'projection'. Awareness of this will reveal how humankind has 'alienated' its own best attributes by projecting them onto an external source: 'the Christian God is Himself just an abstraction from human love', and 'the *secret of theology* is *anthropology*, of the divine being it is the human being'. Criticism of religion 'is destruction of an *illusion*...which...has a thoroughly destructive effect on humankind'. Feuerbach employs an inversion suggested in aspects of early Romantic philosophy, which also occurs in Schelling's critique of Hegel. Idealism, in this view, makes mind the 'subject' and reality the 'predicate'. In idealism, philosophical abstractions are supposed to be the primary reality. (Whether this interpretation is fair to Hegel is questionable, though the way Hegel presents his philosophy can tend to encourage it.) The importance of this idea becomes clear when putatively Hegelian ideas, such as that of 'the state' as the real subject, of which individuals are the predicates, are used to legitimate an unjust, feudal status quo. However, Feuerbach's insistence on sensuous human existence as the prior reality, out of which abstractions are generated, runs the risk of falling prey to Hegel's criticisms of immediacy: as we saw, individual rights cannot exist without mediation through the collective form of the state. This is, though, another case in which considering the issue in purely philosophical terms may obscure the real significance of a philosophical conception. It is Marx who is one of the first to bring this sort of danger to light.

Alienation

The idea that philosophy presents the world in an inverted fashion becomes a crucial issue in 19th-century German philosophy. A feature of modernity is precisely the generation of abstract systems, which have both desirable and disastrous real-world effects. Philosophical concern with the inversion of subject and predicate can therefore also be a manifestation of concrete socioeconomic issues. Like ideas that can be seen as 'ideological', such as some rich people's conviction that poor people are lazy, philosophy can be shown to derive from something not apparent in its conception of itself. An obvious domain where the autonomy of philosophy can be questioned is money. Money abstracts from the concrete things which it enables people to exchange, in a manner analogous to the way a word designating something abstracts from the particularity of the thing in order to make it an instance of a concept. The connection between money and thing, and word and thing, depends on the systematic constitution of the elements in question: a thing's value derives from its being incorporated into a system of discriminations, rather than from anything intrinsic to it. Marx's underlying concern is that such abstractions may have damaging consequences for real individuals, who are essentially particular, whereas systems are general. This contradiction between individual and system creates the space for ideology, when the demands of the system override the needs of the individual.

Marx's key thought is that aggregations of individual human actions lead to unintended systematic consequences. By moving from barter to money exchange, the whole nature of society is transformed, because everything becomes potentially exchangeable for everything else. Critical thought has to understand how such consequences arise, in order to change them for the better. In Marx's early work, of the 1840s, these consequences are seen in terms of 'alienation'. Hegel already used the term to talk about the nature of modernity, and Feuerbach used the term to describe how human attributes are projected onto God. 'Alienation' has been often used since the 18th century to discuss problems of the modern era, from urbanization to industrialization. It is also used to refer to the feeling of not being at home in the world. This sense of alienation depends on the contrast with a time when people supposedly were at home in the world. During most of history, human life has, though, been, in Hobbes's phrase, 'nasty, brutish, and short', so why does alienation seem to be a specifically modern phenomenon? One answer is that it is connected to increases in social mobility: only when there is the possibility of becoming something different can people feel prevented from realizing their true selves. Another answer lies in the changed relationship of humankind to nature. The changes involved here are, though, two-edged. Nature becomes less of an immediate threat, because it can be manipulated to human advantage, but the objectification required for such manipulation creates the sort of gap between humankind and nature that concerned people in Kant's philosophy.

What, then, is the decisive source of the split between mind and nature? There is here already a prophetic tension between an 'ontological' concern with a fundamental 'alienated' way of being, which makes the split into something inherent in human life, and a historical concern that what makes the split occur is human activity, which suggests that, in other circumstances, mind and nature could be reconciled. The former concern demands ways of coming to terms with a necessity which cannot finally be overcome, often leading in the direction of seeing art as a symbolic means of responding to alienation. The latter concern demands a form of secular redemption, in which our relationship to nature becomes a different one, via human intervention.

Marx's early theory of alienation, in the *Economic-Philosophical Manuscripts* of 1844, is more specific than Feuerbach's anthropological conception. Marx sees alienation as inherent in the modern work process. At times, he claims that all 'externalization' of the worker's labour-power involves alienation: 'The object which labour produces, its product, appears against labour as an *alien being*, as a *power which is independent* of the producer'. This conception moves in the 'ontological' direction, in a way in which Marx's most significant work does not: is everyone that produces something for someone else necessarily alienated?

Marx's early work (much of which did not become known until the early 20th century) does, though, contain remarkable insights into the cultural effects of historical forms of labour. Think of how a culture in which the manufacture of material goods is the dominant source of wealth differs from one in which information is that source. His early work, unlike the later work, also carries on the legacy of Schelling. He talks of a society that is fit for human beings as involving 'the true resurrection of nature, the developed naturalism of man and the developed humanism of nature'. This suggests the importance of balancing exploitation of natural resources with the sense that the natural world should not just be subordinated to human needs. In Marx's later work, nature tends just to become the object of human labour. The latter perspective offers little to prevent supposedly Marxist states in the 20th century, like the Soviet Union, producing ecological disaster, of the kind also characteristic of rapacious capitalist economies, by wholly ignoring the independent integrity of the natural world in the name of the satisfaction of often arbitrary human needs.

Ideology and commodity

Marx's mature work in *Capital* (first volume published 1867) seeks to analyse the mechanisms of 19th-century capitalism which lead to the impoverishment of the many in economies that produce ever more wealth for the few. This analysis involves a critical stance towards philosophy. The dominant forms of philosophy, in Marx's view, have an ideological function. Intellectual production is bound up with the ownership of the means of production, and so with the class divisions that are characteristic of capitalism. The 'ruling ideas' are, as he put it in *The German Ideology* of 1845, the ideas of the 'ruling class'. This need not, though, involve conscious deception by those who propagate the ideology which justifies their interests: ideology can function unconsciously.

Were Marx to regard his critique of ideology as a strictly philosophical matter, it would have to explain philosophies wholly in terms of power-relations and forms of production. At times, Marx seems to move in this direction, and this suggests an important problem. *Capital* sometimes presents itself as a scientific account of capitalism, and Marx is prone to adopt the idea that knowing the scientific truth about capitalism is the direct route to achieving the practical political goal of changing it. It is not far from this to saying that society and history are subject to natural laws, and so trying to justify as natural necessity whatever actions are deemed necessary to arrive at a better form of society. Economic factors undoubtedly do create necessities which cannot be avoided: as Marx shows, once a new form of technology renders the previous way of doing things expensive and inefficient, it will generally be adopted. The distance between this historical fact, and the actual ways in which technology affects society – which have ethical and political dimensions – is vital, and Marx sometimes ignores it. His main approach to these issues is via the model of the economic 'base', which causes changes in the social 'superstructure'. The approach can be illustrated by the effects of the move from agrarian to industrial production, which helps bring about the end of feudalism. The specifically philosophical importance of this issue is apparent in his account of 'commodity form'.

Marx attempts to work out an objective measure of value which would allow him to claim scientific status for his theory. However, the key to his theory of value actually undermines this status, and opens up what will be one of his most influential conceptions for subsequent German philosophy. In the Preface to *A Critique of Political Economy* of 1859, Marx asserts that 'It is not the consciousness of men that conditions [*bestimmt*] their being, but, on the contrary, their social being that conditions their consciousness'. A tension is apparent in the word '*bestimmt*', which can mean 'determines', in the sense that a natural phenomenon is causally determined by a scientific law. If '*bestimmt*' is translated as 'conditions', however, it can mean something like 'influences'. This suggests we have a degree of autonomy, even as we are necessarily affected by the sort of society in which we live. Marx talks in this respect of language as 'practical consciousness': language both conditions our consciousness (which means it can function as ideology), and enables us to become in some measure self-determining. The further factor which determines/conditions our consciousness is the commodity form, which, like language, reduces the particular to the general.

In capitalism, the value of something cannot be measured in terms of its intrinsic worth. The latter Marx terms 'use-value'. The highly portable computer I am using has the use-value of enabling me to write this book anywhere that I can work. Its 'exchange value' is expressed by how much I paid for it, or by how much it is worth if I re-sell it: 'As use values commodities are above all of different quality, as exchange values they can only be of different quantity'. The latter value is relational and makes the computer's value equivalent to anything else of the same price. Marx seeks the real basis of value in the average 'socially necessary labour time' required to produce something. If the owner of the means of producing something makes a profit, more of the time taken to produce the thing is worked than is paid to the worker by the owner, who therefore receives unpaid 'surplus value'. This theory has, though, not been a success as an economic tool, and is arguably a moral claim about the unfair distribution of wealth.

What makes the theory of the commodity so compelling to later philosophers, like the Hungarian Marxist Georg Lukács, Heidegger, and Adorno, is its connection to the fate of metaphysics in the modern world. If the aim of metaphysics is a system which can incorporate everything into its terms, the commodity market can be seen as a realization of such a system: any object can be grasped in terms of its exchange value. The system both enables rapid wealth creation and technical innovation, by facilitating the exchange and movement of goods, and has questionable effects on culture: like Oscar Wilde's cynic, it knows 'the price of everything and the value of nothing'. It embodies what made Jacobi see Spinozism as nihilism, namely the way that in the modern world things only are what they are in relation to their 'conditions'. Marx sees both the massive potential of capital to transform the world – he thinks capitalism is a necessary stage of the development of human production, not something to be demonized – and the need to think beyond the commodity form. Jacobi sought a theological basis for value beyond the world of 'conditioned conditions'. Marx thinks of the move beyond this world in terms of political and social revolution, in which the proletariat abolishes the system that oppresses it. Whether that would bring with it the abolition of philosophy depends on how one interprets the goal of philosophy. In the next chapter, we shall consider Friedrich Nietzsche. The difference of Nietzsche's interpretation of the overcoming of philosophy from that of Marx is an indication of historical tensions that will set the scene for philosophy in the 20th century.

Chapter 6

Nietzsche, Schopenhauer, and the 'death of God'

The return of tragedy

The ambivalent nature of modernity is underlined when what Kant and the German Idealists saw as self-determination is suspected of being no more than the disguised instinct for self-preservation. Schelling's and the early Marx's positive revaluation of nature is here replaced by a different kind of 'naturalism', which takes the struggle for existence both as the essence of nature, and as the hidden motivating force of reason. The implications of this questioning of self-determination are most influentially explored in the work of Arthur Schopenhauer (1788–1860) and Friedrich Nietzsche (1844–1900).

Schopenhauer's main work, *The World as Will and Representation* (first published 1818, expanded version 1844), had virtually no effect when it first appeared. It was Richard Wagner's enthusiastic advocacy of the book and the appearance of Darwin's *On the Origin of Species* in 1859, with its devastating implications for humankind's self-image, that helped it to become perhaps the most culturally influential work of philosophy of the 19th century. Indeed, it probably had the most influence on early 20th-century culture too, influencing Thomas Mann, Gustav Mahler, and others. Schopenhauer's *magnum opus* is arguably not a very convincing piece of philosophy, but pointing to flaws in philosophical arguments often fails, as we have seen, to reveal what makes a philosopher's work significant. The most obvious fact about the book is that it is a work of thoroughgoing pessimism and atheism, which introduces a new tragic note into modern philosophy.

German Idealism is admittedly unthinkable without Greek tragedy, but for it tragic necessity is made tolerable by insight into the necessity of change. History may be a slaughter-house, but reason reaches higher stages of development through the bloodshed. The ending of Aeschylus' *Oresteia*, in which a new system of justice emerges from the horror that precedes it, is paradigmatic here. The non-Idealist construal of tragedy to be found in the later Schelling, Schopenhauer, and Nietzsche has, in contrast, no redemptive aspect: human forms of order are overridden by the 'Other'. Think of Oedipus, who unwittingly becomes his father's killer and his mother's husband, or of the devastation of the city by forces from outside it in *The Bacchae*. The pessimistic tragic alternative to the Idealist view is implicit in Schopenhauer's reinterpretation of Kant. Kinship systems, the most basic form of human order, require the sort of identities which are crucial to knowledge. In Kant, perceptual material received from the world only becomes intelligible by being subsumed under categories and concepts in judgements which enable it to be identified with other such material. In Greek tragedy, human forms of identification are threatened with destruction by the fact that the world exceeds what we can know of it. This can, then, be seen as another way of interpreting Kant's 'thing in itself'. The 'excess' of the world over our knowledge leads to tragic situations, in which the kinship order is overriden, leading to incest, matricide, parricide, fratricide, and so on. It is a small step from the idea of this 'excess' to Freud's theory of the unconscious, which was influenced by Schopenhauer. For Schopenhauer, what is manifest, like the ideas of the ego in Freud, is subverted by an unconscious ground. Kant's distinction between 'appearances' and 'things in themselves' becomes that between the world as 'representation' (*Vorstellung*), and the world as 'Will'.

Whereas for Kant there is no access to the world in itself, we have access to the world as Will through experiences over which we have little control, like hunger and sexual urges. Representations are objectifications of the non-appearing 'Will', which is their ground: 'teeth, gullet and intestine are objectified hunger; the genitalia the objectified sex drive'. Schopenhauer terms this ground the 'Will' because, like the 'intelligible' ground of Kantian moral self-determination, it is not part of the spatio-temporal world. However, there is no morality in the Will: it is a blind impulse that constantly opposes itself to itself by throwing up and destroying objective forms. Access to the Will cannot be cognitive, because what we know is the world of 'representation'. This is, then, another case of 'intuition', and it raises again the question of how claims about intuition can be legitimated. How does Schopenhauer *know* that his is a true metaphysical picture of the universe? Once again, however, even if the philosophical point can never be proven, his vision expresses something about the way in which modern humankind relates to the world. Although it is mistaken to reduce philosophy to history, it is nevertheless striking how views of the antagonistic essential nature of reality, from Schopenhauer, to Darwin, to Nietzsche, proliferate at a time when modern capitalism produces an increasingly antagonistic sociopolitical world, which is moving towards the world wars and the Holocaust.

Perhaps surprisingly, Schopenhauer proposes a Platonic view of the timeless essence of the transient, competing objects of the natural world. The influential core of Schopenhauer's vision really lies, though, in its opposition to any sense of natural or human teleology. History is the 'zoology' of the species *Homo sapiens*, not something which moves towards a goal. There is only one way that humankind can escape from the world of eat or be eaten. This is to realize that our awareness of the torment inherent in the Will develops because we are individuated beings. We know of our fragility and mortality because self-consciousness separates us from the rest of reality. This awareness should therefore lead us to seek means of escaping individuation. Schopenhauer is one of the first people in Europe to take non-Western philosophies seriously, and he uses the Buddhist notion of Nirvana to suggest how to escape imprisonment in a world driven by the Will.

Schopenhauer regards aesthetic contemplation as the best, albeit temporary, escape from the real nature of existence. The art that best enables this escape is music, precisely because it is largely non-representational. Music is a direct manifestation of the movement of the Will. His model is the move of a melody away from and back to the tonic: such music echoes how the Will moves from satisfaction, to dissatisfaction, and back. Music uses the source of our dissatisfactions to give us respite from them: it 'does not talk of things, but rather of nothing but well-being and woe, which are the sole realities for the *Will*'. It is this vision which influences Wagner, particularly in *Tristan and Isolde* and the later parts of *The Ring of the Nibelung*. These offer visions of the ultimate futility of human social aspirations that contrast with Wagner's earlier attachment in the 1840s to the idea of redemptive revolution based on love which he derived from Feuerbach.

Apollo and Dionysus

The younger Nietzsche is seduced by Wagner's operatic pessimism, and he sees music as echoing tragedy's presentation of the worst things in the form of aesthetic appearance. His work as a whole, though, exemplifies an ambivalence in modernity's undermining of theology. He moves from a pessimism like Schopenhauer's or the later Wagner's, to the idea that a pessimistic view of life is itself a residue of disappointed theological and metaphysical beliefs. Finding the world to be a terrible place only makes sense if one thinks that there is a true world which is not terrible, in terms of which this world can be judged. If the idea of this true world is an illusion, one should affirm the world we actually live in. The alternative is what the later Nietzsche means by 'nihilism', which is the consequence of losing metaphysical beliefs and failing to accept the consequences. The failure to accept that there is no reason for the terrible aspects of reality generates 'ressentiment', the desire to blame something external for one's situation. Ressentiment is characteristic of what he calls Christian 'slave morality', that seeks a redemption from suffering by the demonstration that suffering has a purpose.

Nietzsche's first major work, *The Birth of Tragedy out of the Spirit of Music* (1871), relies on Schopenhauer's metaphysics, which it translates into a scheme derived from Greek mythology that Friedrich Schlegel and Schelling both already used to symbolize the divided nature of human existence. 'Apollo' stands for the world of 'representation', for anything which can have an identifiable form. 'Dionysus' stands for the Will, in which individuation is dissolved and one 'loses one's self'. Tragedy requires the interaction of Apollo and Dionysus, with music expressing the Dionysian element that words cannot convey. The Dionysian gives rise to constantly changing appearances, while not itself appearing, and has no goal. Nietzsche's later rejection of Schopenhauer is already hinted at, however, in the fact that tragic art is not so much a means of escaping Will-driven existence as a manifestation of creativity which makes life worth living, even though it is ultimately meaningless: 'for only as *aesthetic phenomenon* is existence and the world eternally *justified*'. The *Birth of Tragedy* is the culmination of the elevation of art to metaphysical status in German philosophy. Significantly, this culmination is connected to a radically non-theological, tragic assessment of the meaning of human existence.

Jacobi had suggested that seeing the world wholly in scientific terms, via the 'principle of sufficient reason' – 'everything has a reason/cause/ground' – led to 'the abyss', because it generates an infinite regress of causes of causes. Nietzsche adopts Jacobi's view as a way of questioning the scientific optimism that was a feature of the second half of the 19th century. Those who share this optimism have the 'unshakable belief that thinking reaches into the deepest abysses of being via the leading thread of causality'. Whereas Jacobi uses faith in God as a way of escaping the regress generated by this thread, Nietzsche thinks tragedy is the acknowledgement that nothing rationally grounds existence. His apparently odd claim that without 'art in some form or other, particularly as religion and science', existence is unjustified and intolerable, means that all forms of mental production are 'art', because they project form onto what is otherwise formless.

Calling science an art is, of course, a deliberate provocation. In German philosophy from the middle of the 19th century onwards, philosophers tend either to regard the humanities as inferior to natural sciences, or to seek a method for the human sciences which would make them as rigorous as the natural sciences are supposed to be (see Chapter 7). Nietzsche tries to short-circuit the distinction between science and art by refusing to give priority to any conception of the world: they are all just human ways of dealing with existence. All human conceptions are therefore a kind of myth, and Wagner's revival of myth in his music dramas shows a new, tragic acceptance of the limits of the ability to control existence. The implication is that music may be as good as philosophy at offering insights into the nature of existence. The contemporary world involves a battle, Nietzsche claims, between 'insatiably optimistic cognition and the tragic need for art'. What matters is whether one's actions make one's existence meaningful, even as one faces up to the horrors which it always potentially involves. Because music relates to negative aspects of existence – Schubert once reportedly said that there was no really happy music – it has the same source as tragedy, but it can also be a spur to living on.

Destroying philosophy

Nietzsche does not give up his attachment to the idea of Dionysus. As the God who is torn apart and remade, Dionysus is a symbol of the need to destroy in order to make something new. After the *Birth of Tragedy*, however, Nietzsche begins to question the very aims and assumptions of philosophy itself, which leads him to his own attempts at destruction and renewal. He moves initially, in works like *Human, All Too Human* (1878), to a position more in line with 19th-century 'positivist' optimism about science's ability to answer metaphysical questions. Such radical shifts of position – the *Birth of Tragedy* saw science as just another kind of myth – become typical, and he sometimes makes such shifts within the same text. Nietzsche's refusal to be consistent poses the question of whether logical consistency is the ultimate philosophical virtue, or whether philosophy's aim should be 'performative' effect, influencing the reader's orientation in life in concrete ways. During the 1880s, his questioning becomes more radical, and he produces his most important works, like *The Gay Science* (1882, expanded edition 1887), *Beyond Good and Evil* (1886), *On the Genealogy of Morals* (1887), and *The Antichrist* (first published 1894). He descends into madness in 1889: the exact cause of the madness remains disputed.

Using the assumptions of mainstream academic philosophy to assess Nietzsche can miss the point of what he is doing. However, it is also notoriously difficult to ask radical questions about the aims of philosophy practised in Nietzsche's manner without presupposing much that one wants to oppose. In recent debates about 'theory' in the humanities, for example, Nietzsche-influenced 'post-modernists' are often characterized as 'denying truth'. They see what is held as true, including the best-confirmed theories of natural science, as being a product of the power-relations in a society. It is easy then to ask whether it is true that power-relations determine what is held as true. The post-modernist is manoeuvred into undermining or contradicting themself, because their own assertions about truth will be generated by the desire for power (which would not necessarily invalidate the assertions). This demonstration that we must presuppose truth in the very act of making an assertion can invalidate poorly framed approaches to issues of truth and power. However, although Nietzsche himself can argue in a questionable manner, when he, for example, makes positive claims of the kind that 'truth is really x', such as a 'moving army of metaphors' that we find useful for controlling the world (is this claim itself merely another metaphor?), his questioning can still be revealing.

When traditional authority loses its legitimacy, the issue of ideology becomes inescapable, because people have to try to establish new forms of power to legitimate their actions. This means that conflicts over truth and value in concrete social contexts are always connected to such attempted legitimations, even though the content of claims about truth and value cannot be reduced to what motivates the claims. Nietzsche's perhaps most characteristic contention is that moral concepts are just expressions of changing power-relations in society. He suggests that traditional philosophical attempts to characterize the essence of good and evil can be subverted by showing how very differently the terms are applied in differing historical and social contexts. However, his claims that he is initiating a 'transvaluation of all values' by this approach are very questionable: the Christian values he seeks to undermine seem, in the light of subsequent history, to be more defensible than his alternatives.

Nietzsche's approaches to issues of truth and value sometimes lead to the sense that there is nothing more to truth than the exercise of power over the 'other', be that nature, or other people. As a bald philosophical claim, the contention cannot be defended, but Nietzsche, as we saw, is not necessarily just advancing philosophical claims. In recent times, Michel Foucault has helped to revolutionize the history of science by showing in detailed historical investigations that the key issue is very often *why* people held ideas to be true, rather than what was actually held to be true. History shows that the latter often has a limited shelf-life, even in the natural sciences.

Foucault's investigations are a development of one of Nietzsche's essential concerns, namely with the *value* of truth. The grim side of human existence suggests why asking about the value of truth is important. Do you, for example, really want to know the truth about whether you have a fatal illness for which there is no prospect of a cure? Modern philosophy's obsession with epistemology and answering the sceptic can look questionable because it neglects the ways in which knowing is not always the most effective way of responding to the world. But what is specifically modern about questioning the prior value of truth? In Greek tragedy, knowledge of the truth can already produce, rather than obviate, disaster: think of Oedipus. The early Nietzsche's ideas about the revival of tragedy indicate why he moves in the direction he does. He is, from the beginning, reacting against Platonic and Christian redemptive attitudes to metaphysics and truth, for which the sufferings of this life will make sense in heaven and the true representation of the world is the ultimate goal of knowledge.

Nietzsche's later approach to these issues is brilliantly summarized in a section of *Twilight of the Idols* (published in 1889). The passage in question is not best read as an argument which moves from premises to conclusions about the 'true world'. Its literary 'form' is as important as its philosophical 'content':

> How the 'True World' Finally Became a Fable
>
> History of an Error
>
> 1. The true world is attainable for the wise man, the pious man, the virtuous man, – he lives in it, he is it.
>
> (Oldest form of the Idea, relatively clever, simple, convincing. Re-writing of the sentence 'I, Plato, am the truth'.)
>
> 2. The true world, unattainable for now, but promised to the wise man, the pious man, the virtuous man ('for the sinner, who repents').
>
> (Progress of the Idea: it becomes finer, more seductive, more incomprehensible, – it becomes a woman, it becomes Christian…)

3. The true world, unattainable, indemonstrable, unpromisable, but even as a thought it is a consolation, an obligation, an imperative.

(Basically the same old sun, but through mist and scepticism; the ideas become sublime, pale, Nordic, Königsbergian.)

4. The true world - unattainable? at any rate unattained. And, as unattained, also unknown. Consequently not consoling, redemptive, obligating: to what could something unknown obligate us?...

(Grey morning. First yawning of reason. Cock-crow of positivism.)

5. The 'true world' - an idea which is no longer any use for anything, not even obligating any more, - an idea that has become useless, consequently a refuted idea: let's get rid of it!

(Bright day; breakfast; return of bon sens and cheerfulness; Plato blushes with embarrassment; pandemonium of all free spirits.)

6. We have got rid of the true world: what world was left? the apparent world, perhaps?... But no! with the true world we have also got rid of the apparent world!

(Noon; moment of the shortest shadow; end of the longest error; highpoint of mankind; INCIPIT ZARATHUSTRA.) [Zarathustra is the character Nietzsche employs to convey the idea of the superman who transcends Christian metaphysics.]

Giving a detailed commentary on such a passage is a bit like explaining a joke: it can obscure the effects of the form by trying to explain the content. Nietzsche outlines the moves from Plato's view that the truth of the world lies in the timeless forms of things, not in the way they appear, to Christianity's translation of Plato's vision into the idea of heaven and the afterlife as compensations for the imperfections of this life, to Kant's location of morality in the timeless intelligible realm, to the 19th-century positivist attacks on metaphysical claims in the name of verifiable, 'positive' science, to the realization that philosophy has got in the way of living in the here and now, to the end of metaphysics as the search for one true world. Is it necessary or desirable, though, wholly to abandon the understandings of truth that Nietzsche ironically undermines here? There are two basic interpretations of how to approach Nietzsche's later stances.

One interpretation suggests that Nietzsche offers an apocalyptic transformation of assumptions about philosophy and the world, which would radically change the world. He often gives weight to this interpretation by his intemperate rhetoric, and his reactionary politics, which favour the strong against the weak. In the light of subsequent history, from the world wars to the Holocaust, this interpretation compels one to ask if Nietzsche's work is a causal factor in these shattering events. It is hard to make a consistent connection between the historical events, and his desire for a 'transvaluation of all values' and for the 'superman' who overrides the 'slave morality' of Christianity. There are, though, times when the fact that the Nazis used parts of his work for their purposes have to give pause for thought: 'The Triumph of the Will' cannot help but remind one of Nietzsche.

The other interpretation considers Nietzsche in terms of the need to get beyond philosophy, in order to be able to value the 'ordinary', the bright day and breakfast of 'How the True World'. A related stance will later appear in Wittgenstein's idea that the task is to cure oneself of philosophical anxieties, rather than seek answers to philosophical problems. A key element in non-apocalyptic interpretations of Nietzsche is his 'perspectivism', the rejection of the idea of a 'view from nowhere' which gives access to pure objectivity. However, claiming that there really is no view from nowhere presupposes a location whose existence one is at the same time denying. Another way of trying to articulate Nietzsche's stance is to question the theory that truth is the 'correspondence' of thought or statement to 'state of affairs', 'fact', 'object', or whatever. However, denying this theory (rather than suggesting it may be incoherent or unintelligible) entails the demand for an alternative theory, and this raises the problem of what would make the alternative theory of truth true. There seems to be a necessary circularity in any theory of truth, so the strategy for articulating a convincing version of what Nietzsche might offer has to be a different one.

A more plausible move is to ask whether the correspondence theory of truth itself corresponds to, well, what exactly? If we say 'reality', this is singularly uninformative: we want to know something about the content of what is corresponded to, but that content seems to have to involve the notion of correspondence itself. An arguably unintelligible notion, 'correspondence', is introduced into something which is thoroughly intelligible, namely the everyday sense of truth. We are all familiar with what 'true' means, even though we may not agree on *what* is true: if we weren't familiar with the meaning of 'true', we would not even get to the point of disagreeing. The familiarity at issue here is another case of 'intuition': trying to cash out the familiarity in a cognitive claim always presupposes a prior understanding which cannot be definitively analysed. This point will be vital in Heidegger, and it is not always clear that Nietzsche has grasped it. The basic issue here is how to respond to what appears to be beyond the limits of what philosophy or science can explain. The most obvious case of this issue in modernity is, of course, theology.

After God?

Nietzsche captures the essence of the relationship between theology and modernity in this masterful little section of *The Gay Science: 'New Struggles'*:

> After Buddha was dead they continued to show his shadow for centuries in a cave – a massive eerie shadow. God is dead; but given the way human beings are there will perhaps still be caves for millennia in which his shadow is shown. – And we – we also have to triumph over his shadow!

Overcoming what 'God' meant and means will not happen, for example, via a decisive philosophical argument, or via the advance of science. The 'shadow of God' can just as easily be present in an uncritical atheistic 'scientism', for which the true description of everything in the world, including art and morality, is ultimately reducible to scientific laws, as it can be in traditional theology. In both cases, the assumption is that there is an absolute perspective which enables us to escape our contingency and finitude.

Even the mature Nietzsche quite often fails to follow his own insight here. His idea of the 'will to power', which maintains that there is no self-determining subject, merely manifestations of how one quantum of power gains power over another quantum in some part of nature, is really just another metaphysical vision, akin to Schopenhauer's Will. This is equally the case for his idea of the 'eternal recurrence', which proposes that the universe will keep recurring in exactly the same way in the future – the point being

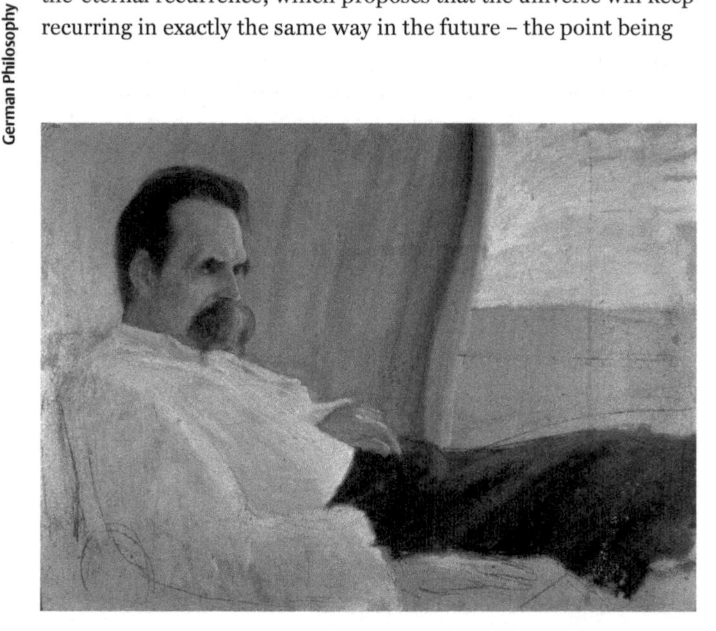

6. Friedrich Nietzsche on his sick-bed, c. 1899, by Hans Olde

that one should affirm life as it is by willing such recurrence. Such theories involve a desire for definitive mastery of what humankind and the world can be understood to be. This desire obscures the possibility that what we are is also what we can become, which leaves us open in both positive and negative ways to contingency. Nietzsche's creative responses to contingency elsewhere in his work are one reason why someone who could be at times a reactionary, anti-democratic misogynist has, for example, also been used in recent philosophy to argue for a democratic culture of self-creation, and to question whether people have an essential gender identity. The underlying philosophical dilemma suggested by Nietzsche's work is, then, that trying to say in a philosophical theory what the world would look like if we were finally to emerge from the shadow of God can itself mean falling under that shadow once again. This dilemma will recur in 20th-century German philosophy.

Chapter 7
Neo-Kantianism, analytical philosophy, and phenomenology

Academic philosophy

The division in contemporary philosophy between 'European/Continental' and 'analytical' philosophy does not exist in the 19th century. It is, however, far from clear what the real nature of this division is, beyond the fact that some, but not all, philosophers from both 'sides' regularly fail to discuss thinkers from the other 'side'. The division is in fact probably best considered as a series of contrasting approaches to modern philosophical questions, rather than as just one issue. One such contrast becomes apparent in the German academic philosophical scene from around the time of Nietzsche until the Nazi takeover in 1933. The relationship to university philosophy of the thinkers we have considered so far varies: some, like the early Romantics, Marx, and the later Nietzsche, did not hold university posts, others, like Schelling and Hegel, did. During the later 19th century, university research, especially in the natural sciences, becomes ever more systematically organized and specialized, and philosophers are increasingly forced to confront questions concerning philosophy's status as a discipline. Is philosophy the key to the natural sciences, or vice versa? Is art or science the primary location of philosophical insight? Contrasting responses to these questions give rise to the sort of divisions now characteristic of the contemporary European/analytical divide.

The main forms of German university philosophy in the period in question are neo-Kantianism, the beginnings of analytical philosophy, and phenomenology. These all seek, in instructively different ways, to establish the role of philosophy in relation to the natural sciences. Why is this their main focus? Hegel's work involved a tension between seeing philosophy as 'its age written in thought', and as the definitive systematic account of the mind/world relationship. The former raises the issue of relativism, of whether what is true is no more than the consensus of a particular culture: if that is the case, it can put philosophy's status in doubt. The latter involves a strong metaphysical claim, which would sustain philosophy's first-order status in relation to the sciences. However, this claim looks less defensible in the face of the growing success of empirical methods in the natural sciences, and it is a feature of philosophical reflection in this period by natural scientists, like Hermann von Helmholtz (1821–94), that they reject Schelling's and Hegel's speculative philosophy.

Given the evident success of the sciences there might seem to be little reason to be overly concerned about epistemological dilemmas, and it is here that one source of the divide in the traditions becomes apparent. Nietzsche and American pragmatism share the idea that questions about the value of truth should often override epistemological concerns. William James suggests that truth is 'the name of whatever proves itself to be good in the way of belief'. What proves itself to be good will vary in differing cultural circumstances, and this takes James's remark in the direction of relativism. However, consensuses about truth often prove to be false, and they are anyway rarely universal. In the German university context, many philosophers came to regard the lack of a definitive philosophical account of scientific truth as pointing to a 'crisis of foundations' in the sciences. If it could be shown that the sciences did need philosophical legitimation, the disciplinary status of philosophy would, of course, be secure. However, there is an ambiguity here, which has considerable consequences for the European/analytical divide. Is the problem really the philosophical underpinning of the truth of the sciences, in terms, for example, of Kant's categories, or of a 'logic of scientific discovery', or is it rather the relationship of scientific to other responses to reality? The former is a crisis of epistemological foundations, the latter of foundations for the aims of modern life. It is not self-evident what the relationship between these two crises really is.

Which Kant?

The ambivalence concerning the crisis is apparent in how Kant is reappropriated in 'neo-Kantianism'. The question of '*Erkenntnistheorie*', 'epistemology', becomes the central focus of thinkers like Hermann Cohen (1842–1918), Paul Natorp (1854–1924), and Ernst Cassirer (1874–1945), who are often termed the 'Marburg School'. Their main concern was reinterpreting Kant's view of philosophy's relationship to the natural sciences in the light of new scientific discoveries, such as Einstein's theory of relativity, though Cassirer in particular would eventually cover much wider issues, in works such as *Philosophy of Symbolic Forms* (1923–9). The chief representatives of 'South West' neo-Kantianism, Wilhelm Windelband (1848–1915), Heinrich Rickert (1863–1936), and Emil Lask (1875–1915), also concerned themselves with epistemology, but they saw Kant's categories in terms of the 'norms' governing the validity of cognitive and other claims. The problem which most highlights the significance of neo-Kantianism appears in Windelband's distinction between 'nomothetic' explanatory inquiry into law-bound phenomena, and 'ideographic' inquiry into understanding individual historical phenomena which cannot be subsumed under general laws.

If philosophy really could provide an account of the conditions of possibility of knowledge, it would be a first-order discipline, and the particular sciences would be second-order disciplines. Neo-Kantianism tries, therefore, to establish philosophy's status by reflecting on the issue of 'conditions of possibility'. That thinking necessarily operates with preconceptions is unexceptional, but are these timeless structures belonging to all rational beings, or are they socially generated evaluations? If they are the latter, do they remain constant, or do they change in differing circumstances? How does the thought that identifies the preconditions relate to the preconditions themselves, without either making dogmatic claims or ending in a regress of preconditions of preconditions? Why not, though, just drop the philosophical baggage, and rely on warrantable science? These questions would have an answer were there a foundation, be it the transcendental subject, or the facts of the best-warranted science, which would define the status of philosophy. (The latter leads some thinkers to the highly questionable idea that the conditions of knowledge should be discovered by the science of psychology.) One side of this dichotomy starts with the subject as foundation, the other with the object. This echoes the situation which led Hegel to try to avoid any 'immediate' subjective or objective foundation, and Windelband, for one, was led later in his career towards the Hegelianism he had previously shunned.

Because the physical sciences offer more and more testable answers to what had been philosophical questions, the 'ideographic' human sciences can appear to lack 'scientific' rigour. Wilhelm Dilthey (1833–1911) therefore demands a 'critique of historical reason', which would establish methods for doing justice to the uniqueness of cultural phenomena. Others, though, come to see truth solely in terms of what can be empirically validated in the sciences, excluding ethics and aesthetics from the realm of truth altogether. In the German context, this attitude is often termed 'positivism'. The coincidence of this extreme view with the appalling destructive potential of the application of the sciences encountered during the First World War and after suggests why some German philosophers will see positivism as dangerously connected to the dark side of modernity. The gap between what the sciences can do, and humankind's ability to use them for the greater good is essential to understanding the tensions in 20th-century German philosophy.

The second 'linguistic turn'

From the vantage point of much of 20th-century Anglo–American philosophy, the important philosophical developments in Germany in the later 19th and early 20th centuries are the ones that will be rather cursorily characterized here. The reasons for being suspicious of the Anglo–American perspective are suggested by the Austrian philosopher Moritz Schlick's claim in 1932 that:

> the fate of all "philosophical problems" is this: Some of them will disappear by being shown to be mistakes and misunderstandings of our language and the others will be shown to be ordinary scientific questions in disguise. These remarks, I think, determine the whole future of philosophy.

This remark could admittedly have been made by the Nietzsche of *Human, All Too Human*. The difference is that Schlick is part of an ideologically driven movement that lacked the later Nietzsche's, admittedly sporadic, realization that one may be still thinking in the 'shadow of God' by trying to come up with definitive ways of obviating 'philosophical problems'. The 'whole future of philosophy' so far has done anything but confirm Schlick's prophecy: some contemporary analytical philosophers are, for example, again trying to provide answers to metaphysical problems. So what went wrong?

The anti-metaphysical aims of many of the German-language founders of analytical philosophy might seem to put them in the same camp as Nietzsche, and some of Schlick's contemporaries, like Otto Neurath, were influenced by Nietzsche (and by Marx). By the 1920s, the sense that there was a need for a philosophy which would use testable science to counter the irrational ideas which were characteristic of fascism was quite understandable. There is, though, no necessary link between the core analytical idea that the problems of philosophy are to be considered in terms of linguistic analysis, and an anti-metaphysical, scientistic stance. Moreover, the basic idea that an understanding of language is central to philosophy was already proposed by Hamann and Herder. It is here that a vital issue emerges, because the thinkers of the first 'linguistic turn' have a very different view of what language *is*. For Hamann and Herder, language is the form of expression of all that it is to be human, which means that aesthetic expressions, for example, can be as important as statements of fact. The difference of their approach from an analytical one becomes apparent if one looks at what becomes the decisive idea about language in analytical philosophy.

This idea is first articulated by a Czech philosopher, Bernard Bolzano (1781–1848). It appears in his claim that the 'objective representation designated by any *word* is, as long as this word is not ambiguous, single'. The inherently particular mental goings-on of any empirical individual cannot be the basis of an account of thought and meaning, because meanings cannot be articulated without language, the general medium for sharing thoughts between individuals. Meanings must, then, somehow be 'in the world': the big question is how this is to be understood. The idea that meanings are in the world might seem to make them the object of a theory analogous to a scientific theory, hence Bolzano's idea that meanings are 'objective representations' designated by words, rather than something contingent and subjective.

The fate of this 'semantic' approach, which forms the core of what can strictly be termed analytical philosophy, turns on the qualification 'as long as this word is not ambiguous'. How does one know when a word is not ambiguous? Presumably this must be established by defining the word's literal meaning. Much of the history of analytical philosophy could, though, be said to consist of failures to do this. If one defines the meaning by using other words, these must in turn be defined by using other words, which threatens a regress of words defining words. Kant had already indicated the structure of the problem here when he argued that judgement could not just rely on the application of rules. If one wishes to 'distinguish whether something belongs under the rule or not, this could only happen via a further rule', which leads to a regress of rules for rules. Moreover, if a first rule is required for learning what meanings are, children would, as Schleiermacher had long since pointed out, have to be able to learn rules even before they knew any words. Given that children do learn language with remarkable facility, the idea that meaning can be defined by learning rules cannot be right. This leads in the direction of the 'pragmatics' of language, the idea that we learn how to use noises to achieve our aims, rather than learn rules of meaning.

The other putative solution to the semantic problem is to have a class of words or utterances whose meaning is somehow 'given' by their very nature. Words which have exact synonyms, and statements which directly point to what they refer to in the world, are two of the candidates for this. As we saw in Chapter 2, the former are what is involved in 'analytic' statements, like 'A bachelor is an unmarried man', which are distinguished from 'synthetic' empirical statements. If, as Schleiermacher already suggested, and Quine argued again in the 1950s, the special logical status attributed to analytic statements cannot be defended, the early analytical project, based on establishing a theory of meaning solely in terms of logical truths and empirical scientific statements, is doomed to failure. Language use must, therefore, be holistic, such that words gain their meaning by their connections to human practices and by their shifting relations to other words. Schlick summarizes the second analytical alternative: 'we must eventually attach words directly to experience in acts of ostension [pointing], and all meaning ultimately resides in the given'. This doesn't work, for the reason indicated by Herder's idea of 'reflection': language enables us to see something as an indefinite number of things. Just pointing to something does not communicate the meaning intended by the person pointing.

Analytical philosophy does not play the main role in 20th-century German philosophy, even though an essential contribution to its development is made by Gottlob Frege (1848–1925). Frege makes groundbreaking advances in logic by moving away from Aristotelian forms of subject-predicate logic, to a 'propositional' logic. The former seems unable to deal with statements like 'Unicorns do not exist', because they have to be analysed such that the predicate existence does not belong to the subject 'unicorn'. In that case, *what* doesn't have the predicate, given that it does not exist? Frege's propositional approach reformulates this in terms of 'There is an x such that x is/is not a unicorn'. Instead of looking for unicorns to see if they can be given the predicate 'existence', one looks, as Ernst Tugendhat has suggested, at what things exist, to see if the description 'unicorn' can be given to them. The value of this approach lies in its ability to account for changes in knowledge, when, for example, what burns ceases to be phlogiston, and becomes oxygen. Frege also introduces a still disputed distinction between 'sense' (*Sinn*) and 'reference' (*Bedeutung*), which he illustrates by the example of the planet Venus. For the ancients, this was two stars, the morning star and the evening star. The reference of these terms is actually the same, but their sense is not. The problem here lies with explicating the notion of 'sense', which has to overcome the problem we saw with Bolzano's 'objective representation', to which it is largely equivalent. Trying to define a sense is faced with the regress-problem described above, which is what leads to the desire for a special class of words whose meaning is unambiguous.

The further development of analytical philosophy in the first half of the 20th century occurs predominantly in Britain and Austria, notably in the work of Bertrand Russell and G. E. Moore, and Ludwig Wittgenstein and the 'Vienna Circle', a group of philosophers and natural scientists who began meeting in Vienna in the 1920s – there is an analogous circle in Berlin, some of whose members, like Hans Reichenbach, would become important in the USA. Their ideas eventually become predominant in many parts of the world, partly because many of the Circle's members were forced into exile by the Nazis, and partly because their assumption that philosophy should be scientific chimes with the growing dominance of the sciences in the academic world. However, the Vienna Circle's project of marrying philosophy and natural science via a theory of meaning is now no longer the major focus of debate in Anglo-American philosophy. (The case of Wittgenstein is complicated, and his work does not play a major role in specifically German philosophy until the 1970s.) It has only been via the work of Ernst Tugendhat and Karl-Otto Apel in Germany since the 1970s that analytical approaches have become important in German philosophical life. Until that time, it is phenomenology which, along with neo-Kantianism, constitutes the main focus of academic philosophy.

Husserl and phenomenology

The importance of phenomenology lies in its challenges to the assumption that causal explanation in the natural sciences will eventually leave nothing for philosophy to do. Analytical approaches undoubtedly narrow the focus of philosophy and exclude much of the complexity of our experience of the world. Theories of time in philosophy, for example, may seek to explain time's essential nature or explain how it relates to space, but these explanations will not necessarily be adequate to the ways in which we experience time. Edmund Husserl (1859–1938) bases his work on the sense that philosophy has not adequately articulated the ways in which the world presents itself to us. These require an approach which shows how we experience time, not as a succession of discrete 'nows', but as a structure of anticipations and retained experiences which constitute the *meaning* of time for us.

Husserl works in a period when 'vitalism', the idea that life either exceeds the concepts we use to grasp it, or is inherently resistant to conceptualization, plays a significant role in cultural life. This is not least because of events such as the First World War, whose unexpectedly cataclysmic nature seems to demonstrate a failure of thought to grasp the nature of modern reality. The philosophical roots of vitalism lie in the question of intuition in Schopenhauer and Nietzsche, and versions of the idea are present in Dilthey, and in thinkers like Ludwig Klages (1872–1956). Significantly, the latter's criticisms of modern rationality and technology in terms of their negative effects on 'life' are accompanied by very questionable political affiliations. Husserl's phenomenology, unlike many vitalist approaches to some of the same issues, seeks new ways of describing experience in philosophy which can be rationally justified, and he comes to realize the wider cultural significance of his approach in the face of the increasingly disastrous development of European history in the 1920s and 1930s.

There is a significant tension in Husserl between a transcendental approach to the basic forms of experience, and a descriptive approach, which becomes increasingly historically oriented in his later work. The tension begins to emerge when Husserl is persuaded that his initial attempts to derive logic and mathematics from laws governing the operation of the mind involve 'psychologism', the confusion of what is established in an empirical discipline with the logical conditions of intelligibility of any science, including psychology itself. The rejection of psychologism brings him closer to Frege and the ideas of analytical philosophy. For the objections to psychologism to be water-tight, however, there must be definitive logical laws, something which Schleiermacher's and Quine's arguments about analytic propositions suggest can be questioned. Husserl's approach is further complicated by his reliance on the idea of the 'natural attitude', which involves experiences that are 'self-evident', or 'originally given', without which meaningful disagreements would be impossible, because these can seem to belong in the realm of psychology.

In order to establish philosophy's independence from natural science, Husserl has to exclude from it all that can be explained in law-bound terms, hence the title of his probably most influential work, *Ideas towards a Pure Phenomenology and Phenomenological Philosophy* (1913). His starting point is 'intentionality', the 'aboutness' of thought, which he analyses in influential new ways. He argues that we must 'bracket' (in what he terms the 'epoché') what we know about an object of inquiry in order to describe the pure structures of consciousness involved in engagement with that object. As many people have since pointed out, from Jacques Derrida on the European, to Michael Dummett and Ernst Tugendhat on the analytical side, this idea is faced with a serious problem as an account of pure internal aspects of consciousness. For the idea to be intelligible, it has to be communicated in language, which is inter- rather than intra-subjective.

Such criticisms have, however, sometimes obscured the aspects of Husserl that are more durable, which influence Heidegger, Sartre, and many others, not just in philosophy. One vital aspect is his offering an alternative to the empiricism that dominated much analytical philosophy until recently, for which 'sense data' are the basic 'given' from which knowledge is supposedly built. Husserl's accounts of perception (there is no single definitive version) stress the fact that experience has to be understood in terms of meanings: every kind of awareness involves a relationship between a mode or modes of attention, and material from the world. The latter cannot be reduced to the former, but without the former there is no way of explaining how it is that we live in a world of immediate significances, rather than the world as seen in the natural sciences. Seeing indeed involves photons hitting the retina, which can be explained in terms of scientific laws, but the experience of seeing something cannot be explained in such terms, and is both prior to and necessary for scientific explanation. Seeing something means that what is seen presents itself as something significant, because we attend to what we need it for, or to what it reminds us of, and so on, none of which are given in the form of photons and retinas.

The importance of Husserl's exploration of how meaning is inseparable from perception becomes most apparent in his 1936 *Crisis of the European Sciences and Transcendental Phenomenology*. In this text, which is influenced by his pupil Heidegger, Husserl moves from what had been a predominantly epistemological approach to the crisis of scientific foundations, to one which sees the crisis as involving the goals of modern life. The crisis in the sciences is reflected in philosophy's failure to address 'questions about the meaning or meaninglessness of this whole human existence'. This failure results from the narrowing of the focus of philosophy which is apparent in aspects of analytical philosophy's tendency towards scientism.

It is here that the important roots of the contemporary divisions between analytical and European approaches become clear. Husserl extends the idea of the 'natural attitude' into the notion of the 'pre- and extra-scientific life-world'. The life-world 'includes within it all actual life, including the life of scientific thought'. Without '*what is a matter of course*... which all thinking, all activity of life in all its purposes and achievements presupposes', the theoretical attitude which characterizes modern science could never develop. The 'theoretical practice' of science is a 'historically late' form of practice. The crisis lies in the fact that this practice comes to dominate all others. Modernity involves a 'mathematization of the cosmos', which Husserl sees as based on changes in the status of geometry. From a practical discipline used for technical purposes in the life-world emerges a discipline concerned with a 'self-enclosed world of ideal objectivities'. This world in turn changes the technology which gave rise to it, by making mathematical exactitude the dominant way of responding to objects in nature, which had previously been seen in more qualitative terms. Nature thus becomes 'a strangely applied mathematics', and the 'arithmetization of geometry' leads to the '*emptying out of its meaning*'. The meaning that is emptied out is not meaning as understood in the semantic project of analytical philosophy, but is rather the way the practice of geometry was woven into the complex life-world which people inhabit. It is here that one can locate the significant content of the analytical/ European divide: the latter sees the semantic project as only one small part of philosophy's proper relationship to modern culture. Husserl himself still attempts to give a transcendental account of the life-world (i.e. an account of the structures which are necessary for it to be constituted in the ways that it is), of the kind he offered concerning the natural attitude, but he is increasingly aware that the pure theoretical account he seeks is threatened by historical contingency. It is Heidegger who reveals the full implications of attempting to sustain philosophy in relation to the particular sciences while confronting the effects of modern history on our descriptions of ourselves and of the world.

Chapter 8
Heidegger

The question of 'Being'

The idea of a crisis in the modern sciences is often questioned on the grounds that, even though Hiroshima, Auschwitz, and other such technologically generated catastrophes could not have happened without modern science, they are a result of the application of science, not of 'science itself'. This claim is usually accompanied by the argument that 'values', i.e. norms for action, cannot be derived from 'facts'. Husserl's account of the mathematization of the cosmos is important because it suggests ways of getting beyond the resulting abstract alternative of something being 'wrong' either with science, or with its application, where exclusive advocacy of either alternative leads to an implausible account of the place of science in the modern world. The point is that the sciences are practices that are inextricably connected to other kinds of practice, all of which require evaluation of what is *worth* doing. This means, as Max Weber argued, that the sciences cannot be self-legitimating, because they do not offer objective criteria for their application, and the unreflective exculpation of 'science' may therefore be an inadequate response to understanding the role of modern science. That the sciences have value because of what they enable that nothing else can enable is unquestionable, but what they enable can also be damaging and destructive. Rather than simply assuming that

7. Martin Heidegger

8. Auschwitz

the main value of the sciences is that they provide a 'view from nowhere', a purely objective theoretical account, then, the prior question is why such a view should be seen as their essential aim. As Husserl argues, the dominance of the mathematically based ideal of pure objectivity is a recent historical phenomenon.

Husserl's move from his more technical work on logic and perception to questions about the very nature of science and modern culture is not least a result of the influence of the ideas of his pupil, Martin Heidegger (1889–1976). Heidegger, in turn, would not have arrived at his ideas without Husserl, but he transforms the ideas he adopts in significant and controversial ways. The complexity of philosophy's relationship to modernity becomes very apparent in the case of Heidegger. He joins the Nazi Party in 1933, seeing it as offering a new approach to the challenges of the modern world for Germany, only leaves it in 1945, and never explicitly apologizes either for his membership or for some of the things he did in the Nazi period, such as denouncing colleagues to the authorities. At the same time, though, his work does offer significant critical means for understanding how the atrocities committed by the Nazis relate to technology's role in modernity.

Why, then, does Heidegger's philosophy remain so important, despite the blatant moral and political failings of its author? Heidegger spends much of his life asking what 'being' means, and he fails to give a definitive answer. Part of the reason is that it is far from clear how the question is to be understood, and the difficulty of clarifying the question is part of its significance. Questions about the 'meaning of being', the '*Sinn des Seins*', must first confront the fact that the meanings of the terms in such questions are not self-evident. The word '*Sinn*' can signify 'meaning', as in the 'meaning of life', which has the connotation of 'direction', 'goal', 'point', or it can just signify what we refer to when we refer to the meaning of a word. '*Sein*' in the title of Heidegger's most influential book, *Sein und Zeit* (*Being and Time*) (1927), could be both a noun and a verb. The meanings of 'to be' or 'to exist' are, moreover, anything but straightforward. Saying that 'life exists on earth', for example, involves a different sense of being from that involved in saying that a predicate belongs to something, as in 'this book is blue', or saying that something is the same as something else, as in 'the morning star is the evening star'. Do these senses have something in common that can be brought under the unitary heading of 'being', or should being be understood precisely as inherently diverse?

The thought which informs Heidegger's explorations is that 'being' means something like 'being intelligible', and things can be intelligible in many ways. We do not emerge into a world devoid of meaning which we subsequently invest with meaning: the world we inhabit is always already meaningful in Heidegger's sense, not least because we have to cope with it to survive. Philosophical questions, like Leibniz's 'why is there something rather than nothing?', which Schelling had begun to develop into the existentialist idea of the contingency of all existence, can only arise if there is already some understanding of what it is for the world to be. The initial task is therefore to characterize such understanding, which Heidegger thinks has been forgotten by Western philosophy. The importance of doing so becomes apparent if one considers an example of the contrasting ways in which we think things are. When we admire the blue sky on a bright summer's day our appreciation of the blueness of the sky will differ from that of a physicist who explains why it is that the sky appears blue. The physicist's explanation can seem like the real basis of what we perceive, which indeed it is, if our aim is to grasp nature as a system of explanatory laws. However, the simple fact that people lived for millennia without warrantable knowledge of why the sky is blue makes it clear that the understanding of being which privileges explanation is not the only kind. Why can't we, for instance, be grateful for a beautiful blue sky, or respond to it in a painting which seeks to capture its blueness, a blueness which is not contained in the colour as an objective fact, but rather in the location of the blueness in a world of significances? The implications of such differing stances become very apparent when some Romantic thinkers warn against the consequences of reducing nature to being just an object to be explained by modern science. Like Husserl in the *Crisis of the European Sciences*, Heidegger sees a distinct role for philosophy in examining the background assumptions and practices without which the objectifications brought about by the sciences would be impossible. Neither of them espouses an 'anti-science' stance: instead, they try to interpret the sciences as offering one way of understanding being, which is not necessarily the ultimate basis of all other kinds of understanding. It is this approach that enables Heidegger to open up vital questions concerning modernity, even as he disastrously misjudges some of its most destructive manifestations.

'*Dasein*' and interpretation

The idea of basic forms of understanding which must precede scientific explanation involves another kind of 'intuition'. Husserl's notion of 'categorial intuition' from his *Logical Investigations* (1900–1) shows why intuition plays a necessary role in this context. We would not be able to investigate objects in the world if we did not understand ways of being which cannot be understood as perceptions of objects. One does not taste the difference between A and B, one tastes A then B. In 'sensuous intuition' one sees the white paper, and A and B; in 'categorial intuition' one understands the paper *as* white, one grasps the relationship or 'state of affairs' 'both A and B'. What words like 'one', 'the', 'and', 'or', 'if', and 'then', 'thus', 'all', and 'none' convey cannot be perceived, but without them we could not understand what we do perceive. The same applies to 'being' which 'is nothing *in* the object, not a part of it': it is '*absolutely not something which can be perceived*'. Husserl's account can be construed as a transcendental reflection on conditions of possibility of knowledge of objects, which puts the emphasis on the subject in the manner of Kant and Fichte. His aim is, though, to get away from the idea of a mind constituting a world, towards a description of how it is that things are intelligible at all, and language is essential to this aim.

Heidegger agrees with Husserl's aims, but he thinks that Husserl's approach still involves the separation of mind and world that leads epistemology to spend its time trying to overcome scepticism. *Being and Time* does expressly argue against scepticism, but the impetus of the book is more a response to the pressure of historical circumstances than an exercise in epistemology. The stripping away of illusions brought about by industrialized warfare, and economic and social disintegration during the First World War and after, demands a new kind of philosophy. It is not so much that philosophy now comes up with better arguments against metaphysics, as that history makes metaphysics, the idea of a timeless true picture of the world, look ever more questionable. Heidegger therefore seeks new ways of characterizing how things are. In doing so, he tries to avoid the use of received philosophical vocabulary, because he regards it as too entangled with the assumptions he wishes to question. He thereby underlines an aspect of the European/analytical divide, of the kind we saw in relation to Hamann: the language of *Being and Time* is inseparable from its content, in a way which will later be the case for the work of Jacques Derrida and others who seek to question the dominant aims of Western philosophy.

Being and Time is best approached via its central term, '*Dasein*', literally 'existence', which has the sense of 'being there/here'. *Dasein* is what we are. However, if one assumes that it therefore means 'human being', one has then to define human being, so raising contentious anthropological questions that are secondary to the real philosophical questions. By stripping away received assumptions about being human, Heidegger arrives at a masterly minimalist characterization, namely that *Dasein* 'is concerned in its being *with* this being'.

Instead, then, of starting with a conscious subject confronted with a world of objects, which raises epistemological questions concerning how the two connect, Heidegger refers to 'being in the world' as the mode of existence of *Dasein*. Our concern is with the things in our world through which we realize our projects. When I type this sentence on the computer, I think about the computer objectively only in so far as I am using it as an example to explain Heidegger's approach, not as the thing I am using to type this sentence. The latter practical concern involves a specific temporality, because it is future-directed. Our engagement with things need not, then, be primarily based on the idea of what they essentially are, but rather on what we aim to do with them. Heidegger uses the example of a hammer: when we use a hammer, it belongs in a practical world in which we put up shelves, and suchlike. It is usually only if the hammer breaks or is the wrong hammer for the job that we apprehend it in objectifying terms, rather than just unreflectively using it. When we objectify it, we realize how the hammer belongs in contexts which often become manifest only when they are disrupted: in Heidegger's terms, the hammer moves from being 'ready to hand' ('*zuhanden*') to being 'objectively present' (*'vorhanden'*). This sort of shift has to do with how we develop the objectifying approach to the world required for scientific investigation.

By giving a 'phenomenological ontology' of 'average *everydayness*', Heidegger shows how theoretical forms of thought derive from practical ways of being in the world, in what he calls a 'hermeneutic of *Dasein*'. Our very way of being is interpretative: as soon as we deal with something in the world in a specific way, we employ the 'As-structure of understanding'. This structure puts in question the idea that things have essences that are always present when the thing is present. What things are manifest as depends instead on the shifting contexts and practices in which they are located. The key issue is the relative priority given to differing kinds of apprehension. Heidegger deals with this issue in terms of the difference between 'being' (*'Sein'*) and 'entities' (*'Seiendes'*), which he refers to as 'ontological difference'. *Dasein* can be the object of anthropological, biological, historical, and many other 'ontic' kinds of investigation as an entity, but these are all derived from the 'ontological' fact that *Dasein*'s being must already be open to question. Without *Dasein* becoming an issue for itself in the first place, the idea that genetics, to take a currently popular example, should be the essential source of our self-understanding could not even arise. Ontological investigation is not intended to invalidate the results of the sciences, but rather to discover their practical and other 'conditions of possibility'.

Being and Time is least convincing when it seeks to give a definitive repertoire of the ways of being of *Dasein*, such as 'Angst' and 'being to death'. Heidegger fails here to take sufficient account of the variations in cultural and historical responses to human existence and mortality, and adopts attitudes which can be seen as particular to the troubled Weimar Republic, rather than as universal ways of being. *Being and Time* offers more productive resources via its explorations of how the understanding of being relates to time. His most controversial philosophical ideas here concern the notion of truth. Does the truth about something which emerges at a specific time entail that what is now seen as true has always been true, even though it was previously not accessible? In so far as 'true' in the semantic sense does not mean 'true for now, but was not true before now, and may be revised later', it is implausible to argue that Newton's laws were not true before they were discovered. However, Heidegger's insistence that the truth comes about in time via our interactions with the world, and so cannot be assumed to be something timeless to which our sentences will eventually correspond, raises vital issues concerning how truth actually 'happens' in the world. As the contemporary German philosopher Albrecht Wellmer suggests, truth seems both to be discovered (which suggests it was already there), and to be produced (which suggests it cannot be there until it is produced). The philosophical attempt definitively to resolve this ambivalence runs the risk of allowing philosophy to obscure how understandings of truth in a rapidly changing world cannot be reduced to a purely semantic perspective. The significance of the question of being lies in the idea that specific claims to truth which can be granted or denied assent only make sense in relation to a prior background of linguistic and other practices which 'disclose' aspects of the world. Without a socially generated repertoire of responses that emerge in relation to what concretely concerns *Dasein*, the particular practice of giving and assessing reasons remains merely abstract.

The 'turn'

Heidegger's development of his philosophy after *Being and Time* is initially best approached via the essay *The Origin of the Work of Art* of 1935. The fact that the essay is primarily concerned with truth in relation to art, rather than science, suggests why there is a deepening divide between this kind of approach to philosophy, and what is happening at this time in the analytical tradition. In *Being and Time*, 'world-disclosure' derived predominantly from *Dasein*'s ways of coping with the world. In the essay on art, it is the artwork itself that makes things manifest. Rather than representing the world, art makes things intelligible in new ways: think, for example, of how Impressionist paintings can change how one sees reflections in water, or how Proust's novel adds new dimensions to how one experiences time. If one thinks of art's rendering things manifest in relation to language, the outlines of Heidegger's later position begin to emerge.

A Heideggerian answer to the familiar modern question of how to establish whether something is art or not would be that art 'happens' when a world or an aspect of a world is disclosed by a work. Heidegger uses the example of a Greek temple, which gives meaning to the world of the community in which it is located. The temple establishes a realm of truth by focusing the activities of the community in a way which transcends any individual intentions of its builders. In an analogous fashion, Heidegger will come to see language as the 'house of being': it must shelter things and give them a place in the world, which is what allows them to be manifest in their truth. But what distinguishes a revelation of truth from a failure to reveal truth, given the many differing ways in which we can say how things are? What is at stake here is suggested in his remark that 'science is not an original happening of truth but in each case the extension of a realm of truth which is already open'. The question is how to interpret the idea of such a realm of truth.

Heidegger's initial idea is already present in Schleiermacher's insistence that science is only possible on the basis of the pre-scientific understanding of natural language. However, does the language that opens the realm of truth constitute a fixed horizon of possibilities, or is it something which can be altered by human practices and critical evaluations? The later Heidegger talks of the history of the major philosophers from Plato to Nietzsche as involving the 'words of being', in the dual sense of words which disclose being and words which emerge from being itself. It is not the contingent (and often now inaccessible) intentions of these philosophers that constitute the philosophical truth of the texts, but rather the way in which they establish how the world is interpreted in an era. He also regards the work of certain key poets, like Hegel's friend Friedrich Hölderlin, as speaking the words of being. Heidegger's later work involves a 'turn' from *Dasein* as the locus of the world's intelligibility, to language in the sense at issue here as that locus. In so far as we do not invent language, which 'happens' to us as we emerge into the world, one can see what he might mean. Heidegger also talks of the 'clearing', in the sense of a clearing in a forest, to convey the idea that the world must be open to us in a manner beyond our control before we are able to reflect on it and objectify it. The problem we saw in Chapter 2, that any attempt fully to grasp language in philosophy would require an impossible perspective outside language, also suggests why Heidegger develops an approach in which the essential relationships to the world are not in the power of the subject. The problem is that his story of 'happening' of language as the words of being tends to become monolithic, equating the history of philosophy with history in general, and human agency seems to play no essential role in it. Heidegger has notoriously little to say about ethics, and the suspicion that his later stance may function as a way of shifting the blame for his moral and political failures is sometimes hard to resist.

It is, however, a mistake to write off Heidegger's later work, despite its obvious deficiencies, because it poses serious questions about the direction of modern philosophy. We encountered the idea of the 'end of philosophy' when looking at Marx. Heidegger develops the idea in a way which connects many of the themes of the preceding chapters. The key is once again the relationship between philosophy and the sciences: 'The development of the sciences is at the same time their separation from philosophy and the establishment of their independence. This process belongs to the end/completion [*Vollendung*] of philosophy'. One of the striking aspects of 20th-century German philosophy is how questions about metaphysics lead in such completely opposed directions. For the Vienna Circle, the advance of scientific explanation reveals metaphysics to be nonsense, which points in the direction of the remarks by Moritz Schlick cited in Chapter 7, where science is seen as eventually abolishing metaphysics. For Heidegger, modern science is *itself* the culmination of Western metaphysics, so metaphysics has exactly the contrary meaning. How can one make sense of such a divergence?

In Heidegger's story, the aim of metaphysics is to explain being, and in modernity this aim is achieved by the sciences. Where, then, does this leave philosophy? The answer involves a further element in Heidegger's story, which relates to another recurring theme in the preceding chapters, namely the tension in the interpretation of subjectivity, that was already apparent in Kant and Fichte, between the subject as finite and dependent, and the subject as the absolute condition of the world being intelligible at all. Heidegger comes to regard the history of metaphysics in modernity as the growing domination of being by the subject, hence the idea that modern science's increasing technological command over nature is the culmination of metaphysics. The consequence is that he thinks that what he is offering can no longer be philosophy, philosophy having revealed itself as what 'subjectifies being'. Whereas previous philosophy can be understood as the attempt to find the ground of subjectivity (in Nietzsche, for example, this is the 'will to power'), Heidegger seeks an alternative that will no longer involve trying to dominate being.

Heidegger's alternative is rather indeterminate, often relying on an inflated view of the possibilities of non-instrumental poetic language for disclosing a new understanding of being that 'lets things be' by 'listening' to them, rather than determining them conceptually, but it can also be illuminating. The title of the essay 'The End of Philosophy and the Task of Thinking' (1969) summarizes how he sees the alternative: if metaphysics and philosophy have become modern science, what sort of thinking can understand what the sciences cannot explain, because it transcends what their methods permit? The world the sciences produce via the application of technology (which he describes as the 'enframing' of being) is the result of ever-increasing specialization. This means that it is impossible to grasp what the cumulative effects of such specialization will be: that is the – perhaps impossible – task of 'thinking'. Heidegger controversially asserts that 'science does not think'. He means by this, for example, that physics cannot finally tell us what physics is. Physics depends on a particular understanding of being, which cannot legitimate itself in its own terms, as there are many other ways of relating to nature. In the face of the growing ecological crisis and the realization of the limits of the Earth's resources, this kind of perspective looks less questionable. It forces us to see how different understandings of being interact to produce something that no single kind of understanding can grasp. Even if Heidegger offers few practical indications of how things might be changed for the better, he does offer alternatives to the kind of philosophy which is so beholden to the sciences that it no longer asks questions about the limits of a scientific understanding of existence.

Chapter 9
Critical Theory

Totality

The economic crash of 2008–9 strikingly illustrates a key issue in 20th-century Marxist theory, which is central to what is known as 'Critical Theory'. What the crash showed was that individual agents or groups of agents could regard their actions as thoroughly justifiable and rational, while the actual collective results of their actions were catastrophic. It does not take much to suspect that the idea of buying more and more debt might at some point come up against the need for the 'credit' (which, of course, means 'belief') to have some basis in real things: so why did so few people realize what was happening? The analogous event that was decisive for the emergence of Critical Theory was the First World War and what came after it. The war was initially greeted by some intellectuals, like the very talented philosopher and sociologist Georg Simmel (1858–1918), and many other people, as a welcome way out of a supposedly decadent society, but resulted in the horrors of the trenches and the attendant economic, political, and social breakdown.

We saw in Chapter 8 how Heidegger was influenced in *Being and Time* by the way historical reality made many academic approaches to philosophy seem redundant. It is likely that Heidegger was familiar with *History and Class Consciousness*

(1923) by the Hungarian philosopher Georg Lukács (1885–1971). In this text, Lukács connected the gap between how people thought about reality and what was really happening to the epistemological dilemmas of the relationship between subject and object. Incorporating aspects of Hegel's questioning of a dualism of subject and object, and Marx's theory of commodity, Lukács sought to understand how modern capitalism itself leads to a subject/object split.

It should already be clear that, as for Heidegger, the kind of sceptical problem concerning the reality of the 'external world', familiar from Descartes, that is still taught in philosophy classes today, is not primarily what is at issue here. So why does Lukács link what he is doing to the epistemological tradition at all? (The book considers Kant and German Idealism as key to its concerns.) In Lukács's terms, the important question is why modern attention to scepticism emerges along with nascent capitalism. The standard objection here is that one risks reducing a philosophical issue to the historical factors in its genesis. However, the change in social relations associated with the rise of modern individualism and new ideas about human autonomy clearly do render people's relationship to the world and other people more complex and indirect, because they rely less on received authority as a stable framework of judgement. Shakespeare's plays are, for example, often concerned with sceptical suspicions which lead people into disaster, as their trust in the world and other people dissolves. The fact that problems about the reliability of cognition only become widely linked to emerging questions concerning self-consciousness in the 17th century makes it clear, as the critical theorists will argue, that history and philosophy cannot be neatly separated.

The key terms in this context, which are crucial to the genesis of Critical Theory, are 'reification', the turning of relations between human beings into relations between things, and the idea of 'totality'. The answer for Lukács to how an event like the war might in future be avoided is to get beyond the situation in which the individual actions of people produce something which they have no means of comprehending. His idea, following Marx, is that the move to capitalism from feudalism brings about the integration into a totality of what were previously unconnected aspects of social and political life. This happens via the commodity structure, which, as we saw in Chapter 6, makes all things into potentially identical exchange values. The totality in question produces reification, which makes people lose sight of the impact of what they do on other human beings. Lukács thinks that the proletariat, the class which, because of the deprivation it suffers, has least reason to be deluded about the system in which it is located, is the key to grasping the totality. By engaging in revolutionary practice, the proletariat has the potential to overcome the conditions which damage the qualitative aspects of their relationship to the world, so creating more humane circumstances. In the light of subsequent history, the fact that, according to Lukács, the proletariat needs the help of the Communist Party to arrive at its solution to the subject/object split makes it clear, however, that there may be no easy solution to the dilemmas he seeks to resolve.

Salvaging radical thought

Critical Theory develops in the face of the failure of the kind of revolutionary response to the disasters of modern capitalism proposed by Lukács. Founded in Frankfurt in 1923 at the height of the post-war German economic crisis by the Marxist entrepreneur Felix Weil, the 'Institute for Social Research', which is often termed the 'Frankfurt School', sought to promote radical social research. As developments in the Soviet Union and the rise of Nazism destroy hopes for revolutionary change, the need to keep progressive ideas alive becomes more pressing, and yet ever more difficult. Theodor W. Adorno (1903–69) and Max Horkheimer (1895–1973), the most important philosophical representatives of the School, adopt much of the analysis of how capitalism affects the very nature of human thought from Lukács's account of commodity and reification. They are, however, forced to find ways of explaining why radical attempts at political transformation may make things even worse. In doing so, they adopt ideas from Freud, to explain people's susceptibility to authoritarianism; from Max Weber, to understand how the modern world functions more and more in terms of rationalization of traditional practices into standardized bureaucratic and technical forms; and from Nietzsche, to criticize the inadequacies of traditional philosophy. The other key influence on Adorno – Horkheimer is more sceptical – is the work of his friend Walter Benjamin (1892–1940).

More than that of any other figure we have encountered so far, Benjamin's work resists being summarized. His work draws on ideas from, among many other sources, Hamann and early Romantic philosophy, Jewish mysticism, and Marxism, and is formidably learned. Two essential, connected themes

9. Theodor W. Adorno, 1960

inform his work: the nature of language in modernity, and the problem of modern temporality. He has a radical sense both of the arbitrariness of language in the modern world and of the transience of modern existence, and yet at the same time looks for what could redeem both language and time. In his earlier work, until his adoption of elements of Lukács's, Brecht's, and others' Marxism from the end of the 1920s, his hope is for some way of coming to terms with the 'disenchantment' that Max Weber sees as the core of modernity. This would happen via an approach to language that would restore its ability to connect to the particular truth of things (which Benjamin thinks of in residually theological terms). His ideas are echoed both in aspects of writers like Hofmannsthal and Rilke, and in the later Heidegger's view of the language of poetry as allowing particular things to be in their truth, rather than classified as examples of general concepts.

Benjamin's step from his earlier view of language to a view informed by Marxism is made possible by linking what he interpreted, particularly in *The Origin of the German Play of Mourning* (1928), as the 'fall' of language in modernity, to the commodity system. Just as exchange value abstracts from the unique particularity of things, language in the modern world has no essential relationship to the things it designates. In his work in the 1930s on the 19th-century French poet Charles Baudelaire, Benjamin says that 'The specific devaluation of the world of things which is present in the commodity is the foundation of the allegorical intention in Baudelaire'. Allegory is the modern manifestation of language's falling away from the world, and it is echoed in the way the world of commodities creates a 'phantasmagoria' – Benjamin sees this exemplified in the shopping arcades that are built in 19th-century Paris – which conceals the brutal reality underlying that world. His judgement may be extreme, but the subsequent development of the world of commodities, which relies on the creation of ever-renewed demand by the attaching of fantasy images to the most banal objects produced in often inhuman circumstances, has done little to invalidate the direction of Benjamin's criticisms.

10. Readers choosing books that are still intact among the charred timbers of the Holland House library, London, 1940

Benjamin's concern with time and history involves exploration of how the past might not just be a dustbin in which everything is lost and becomes meaningless: his ideas on this are presented in concentrated form in his last text, 'On the Concept of History' (1939). The text is influenced by Freud's therapeutic attempts to enable victims of traumatic events to redeem the past which destroys their ability to live in the present. However, Benjamin wishes to transfer this model from the level of the individual to the level of the oppressed collective. Traditional historiography is for Benjamin the history of the victors, which can only reinforce the futility of the past for the victims. Only by a different approach to historical time, which adopts new forms of presentation of history, such as montage of apparently disparate and insignificant historical material, of the kind he collects in his project on the Paris arcades, can one glimpse how aspects of the past might redeem the present. History is, Benjamin contends, a cumulative disaster, a kind of nightmare from which humankind can only awake by changing its relationship to past injustice and oppression, and so radically transforming the nature of society. This stance leads him to reject any linear sense of historical development as adding to the catastrophe, which can only be interrupted by grasping repressed alternatives from the past and connecting them to revolutionary struggles in the present. Given the bleak times in which he is writing, this desperate search for new sources of hope is all too understandable, but reliance on the idea of a total revolutionary transformation of history tends in other circumstances to obscure the more modest ways in which social progress can, despite all, be achieved. Benjamin's tragic death, fleeing the Nazis, meant he could never get to the point of developing a workable political strategy based on his ideas.

Dialectic of Enlightenment and negative dialectics

Benjamin dies before the worst of the historical catastrophe in Europe is over. It falls to Adorno and Horkheimer to try to produce philosophical responses to totalitarianism, the Second World War, and the Holocaust. Towards the end of the War, in exile in the United States, they write *Dialectic of Enlightenment* (*DoE*), which is published in 1947. The task they set themselves is 'no less than finding out why humankind, instead of entering into a truly human condition, is sinking into a new kind of barbarism'. Whatever its faults, the tradition from Kant and Hegel to Nietzsche that leads to Critical Theory makes questions like this the essential task for modern philosophy, rather than the narrow technical questions of much of the analytical tradition.

One of Benjamin's key ideas is that culture and barbarism go hand in hand, and that the most modern technological developments can actually be a manifestation of 'primitive history': the question is how to use such ideas in relation to the real events. One dilemma in dealing with the worst catastrophes of modern history is that received modes of ethical or social explanation seem simply inadequate. Despite the dangers of belittling how bad the man was, Hannah Arendt's contentious phrase about the 'banality of evil' in relation to Adolf Eichmann captures the sense that justified moral condemnation of the man does not get to the root of what happened via his actions. The circumstances that made the Nazi genocide possible involve so many elements, such as bureaucratic rules or technical matters like transport systems, which can seem morally neutral to the people involved in them. *DoE* tries to show that 'Enlightenment', which is the source of the technological and organizational power which enables humankind to control so much of the social and natural world, inherently turns into its opposite, 'mythology'. Enlightenment – which is therefore not just the specific historical phenomenon beginning in the 17th or 18th centuries, but rather is essential to all human culture – is the attempt of humankind to overcome the threat posed by nature to its self-preservation. It is consequently both an ineluctable necessity, and the source of even greater threats to that self-preservation. This dialectical status of Enlightenment is the philosophical contradiction which the book confronts: how does one use reason to assess the fact that reason can be the source of the oppressions one is trying to overcome? In certain respects, *DoE* echoes Heidegger's account of modernity as the subjectification of being, when it talks of 'the subjection of everything natural to the arrogant subject'. However, it is not clear that this philosophical judgement is adequate to the complexity of the historical issues.

DoE and Adorno's subsequent work regard the modern world, in the light of the failure of the increase in knowledge and technical control to reduce the threat of barbarism, as a 'universal context of delusion'. This poses the question of how, if delusion is universal, this description itself avoids being deluded. Adorno does not seek to avoid this contradiction: certainty that one's philosophical analysis is not deluded is precisely likely to lead to delusion. The underlying thought is that philosophical thinking itself has to be questioned, precisely because abstract conceptualizing can be

11. Albert Speer and a model of Berlin

linked to the effects of the commodity structure's abstraction from the particular reality of things. This means that all one can do is engage in specific critical analysis of significant areas of society and culture.

The key for Adorno is to bring out how contradictory modern experience is: his reflections on how to understand freedom in his 1964–5 lectures on history and freedom best exemplify this approach. The aim is not to come up with a philosophical decision between free will and determinism, but rather to show why the issue of freedom cannot be reduced to an answer to a yes/no philosophical question. However, this self-critical attitude, which

Adorno terms 'negative dialectics' (on which he publishes a book in 1966) because, unlike Hegel's dialectic, it does not have a final resolution, is not always consistently maintained. *DoE*'s influential analysis of the 'culture industry', subtitled 'Enlightenment as Mass Deception', looks, for example, at how innovation in the arts can be stifled by the pressures of the market. With respect to large amounts of modern culture that is produced in order for it to sell in as large quantities as possible, the analysis is probably even more apt now than when it was written. However, the claim that such 'mass culture' is inherently deceptive needs to be backed up by detailed empirical investigation, and when the idea is applied to jazz, for instance, it is clearly mistaken. That jazz, like other forms of modern art, is often damaged by commercial considerations is beyond doubt, but its capacity to oppose dominant cultural habits remains intact even today.

Adorno himself seems in certain respects to fall prey to the idea of the totality which he sees as the source of many of the ills of modernity. The aim of understanding how fundamental structures of modern life, which reduce the particularity of things and people in order better to control them, are the source both of smooth-running public services, and of the possibility of efficient mass murder in the extermination camps, is clearly vital. However, when this approach gets reduced to the idea that the world is dominated by 'identity thinking', which has its roots in the equivalences created by the commodity structure, too much can go missing. His extreme stance with regard to questions of identity is what leads Adorno to his implausible inflation of the philosophical importance of certain kinds of modern art. Adorno's best reflections in *Aesthetic Theory* (1970) make it clear how important art's resistance to being reduced to something that can be definitively known is for modern philosophy. At the same time, his insistence that only the radical modernism epitomized for him by Schoenberg, Beckett, and Kafka avoids the snares of the culture industry and tells the truth about modernity can be almost as reductive as what he is opposing.

Language and rationality

The 'Economic Miracle' which saw West Germany recover from comprehensive moral, political, and economic ruin during the 1950s allowed a great deal of repression of the past. Until the criticisms of continuities between the Nazi period and the Federal Republic by the Student Movement towards the end of the 1960s, Adorno's dogged insistence on the need to come to terms with the Nazi past was anything but the norm. Adorno's uncompromising philosophical stance did, however, seem to leave insufficient space for how to think concretely about necessary social and political reforms in a world not so immediately threatened with catastrophe. His pupil, Jürgen Habermas (1929–), the most influential post-war German philosopher and social theorist, therefore sought to salvage a more constructive conception of rationality than seems possible with the assumptions of *DoE*. His claim is that *DoE* works with a conception of rationality as

12. Jürgen Habermas and Joseph Ratzinger, January 2004

something purely instrumental, which excludes its communicative basis. In essence, Habermas wishes to show that a Nietzschean conception of rationality, based on the subject's drive to dominate the object, has no room for the fact that interpersonal communication can involve the renunciation of power, when a subject encounters the 'forceless force of the better argument' of their interlocutor.

Habermas tries to use an new understanding of 'communicative action' to give philosophy a role in the workings of democratic societies. In doing so, while engaging with analytical philosophy, he adopts aspects of American pragmatism, which does not aim at an account of the nature of thought's representation of reality, but rather at an account of human action as the primary way in which we relate to the world. He outlines what he terms, following his colleague Karl-Otto Apel (1922–), a 'transcendental pragmatism'. Pragmatic 'conditions of possibility' are not forms of thought, but 'structures of experience and action'. Arguments about validity of all kinds, cognitive, moral, and aesthetic, are carried out in social life via these structures: without them it is unclear how disputes about validity could arise at all. The structures do not give priority to the natural sciences because there is no privileged form of access to the objects of scientific knowledge that can be validated outside of communication about those objects. The crucial factor in all claims to validity is therefore the social process of argumentation.

A key influence on Habermas is Heidegger's pupil Hans-Georg Gadamer, who, in *Truth and Method* (1960), had aimed to 'seek out the experience of truth which exceeds the realm of control of scientific method . . . and to interrogate it as to its own legitimation'. This involved an extension of Heidegger's version of hermeneutics, in which our primary way of being is interpretative, rather than cognitive. Gadamer thinks one has to rehabilitate the notion of 'prejudice', because without prejudices, in the form both of language and of all the ways in which we are always already unconsciously affected by and cope with the world, we could not reach the level of objectifying reflection in the sciences. Following the Romantic tradition and the later Heidegger, Gadamer gives a central role to art in questioning the dominance of the methods of the natural sciences. The artwork is not something to be determined by concepts, but something which 'happens' via its reception in real social contexts: 'understanding is never a subjective relationship towards a given "object", but belongs rather to the effective history, and that means: to the being of that which is understood'. Because we can never finally step outside the 'traditions', in the sense of that which is carried across time, in which we are located, the metaphysical aim of a view from nowhere is seen by Gadamer as a questionable illusion that can have damaging consequences for culture. It is not that scientific methods are mistaken – he thinks the sciences involve an unstoppable dynamic which cannot be halted by philosophical or other objections – but:

13. Hans-Georg Gadamer

> this does not mean that people would be able to solve the problems that face us, peaceful coexistence of peoples and the preservation of the balance of nature, with science as such. It is obvious that not mathematics but the linguistic nature of people is the basis of human civilization.

Gadamer rejects positive metaphysical claims, in the name of the inescapability of dialogue in dealing with matters of truth and validity, and, in the light of Gadamer's contentions, Habermas comes to reject his initial hopes for a theory which would definitively show how communication can be distorted by power and lead to 'false consciousness'. We can never achieve a fully objective viewpoint on cultural practices and forms of communication, because we are always already situated within the prejudices of a culture. This does not mean that one renounces the idea of a Critical Theory for an uncritical relativism, but the theory now has to be developed in terms of 'post-metaphysical' inter-cultural dialogue.

The key problem, which has led Habermas in more recent work to concern with international law, is how, in a globalized world, to arrive at universal legal and other norms while doing justice to locally developed cultural norms. He initially looks for universals in forms of communication, suggested by his notion of the 'ideal speech situation'. The very fact of arguing about validity involves a 'telos of agreement': otherwise it would just be a matter of exerting power over one's interlocutor. Although real communication always involves some strategic exercise of power, the idea of allowing oneself to be persuaded by the better argument seems to suggest that we can imagine ideal conditions of communication. Habermas moves away from this notion, however, because it is essentially abstract. One can never know whether one is engaged in ideal conditions of communication or not, because, as Gadamer's arguments had implied, that requires a location outside the real practice of communication. He does not, though, give up on the attempt to sustain a strong conception of rationality based on the forms of validity which are inherent in everyday communication in the life-world.

The question is what role philosophy should play, given Habermas's assumption that, in the light of past failures, the more emphatic metaphysical aims of modern philosophy should be renounced. He suggests, adopting Kant's division of the modern domains of science, of law and morality, and of art, that philosophy might now 'at least help to set in motion again the frozen interplay between the cognitive-instrumental, the moral-practical and the aesthetic-expressive, which is like a mobile that has become stubbornly entangled'. Every facet of Habermas's conception has been subjected to often justified philosophical criticism, but the durability of his vision lies in the appropriateness of its democratic response to the nightmares of Germany's past. For all its faults, Germany is now one of the world's more open democracies, and Habermas has made a substantial contribution to what made this possible.

Contested heritage

The post-war German philosophical landscape has involved versions of all the directions in philosophy looked at in the preceding chapters. The emphasis here on Critical Theory and Gadamer's hermeneutics is based on the fact that the debates to which they gave rise were most important for wider social and political issues in the modern world. German philosophers have generally had to face a tension between extending and critically assessing the tradition from Kant onwards, and seeing how philosophy can be used to address pressing social and political matters. The former has the tendency to lead to a rather scholastic concern with the detail of historical texts, the latter is always faced with the contingencies involved in dealing with complex social and historical realities. Somewhat strangely, the period leading up to and following the major changes in 1989 was not characterized by a plethora of responses on the part of German philosophers.

With the exception of established older figures, like Habermas and Dieter Henrich (1927–) (who is notable for his combination of outstanding scholarship and concern for philosophy to address vital contemporary issues), German philosophers tended to retreat from political *engagement*. Moreover, at the very moment when, in the United States, many leading philosophers, like Richard Rorty, John McDowell, and Robert Brandom, were suggesting that the analytical tradition was in need of resources from Kant, Hegel, and Heidegger if it was both to come up with new responses to key philosophical issues and play a wider role in cultural politics, some younger German philosophers were rejecting the German tradition in the name of often quite narrow, technical versions of analytical philosophy.

As the German tradition has repeatedly shown, understanding philosophical movements is not necessarily a matter that is purely internal to philosophy. Both the sense of political and social disorientation in Germany in the wake of 1989, and the realization that the rising prosperity which was related to the emergence of radical thinking from the later 1960s onwards may well be a thing of the past, have something to do with many younger German philosophers' retreat into specialization, but it is not yet clear precisely what. At the same time, the tradition which they now regard with suspicion offers possibilities we have encountered in Schelling, Heidegger, Adorno, Habermas, and others, for responding to many of the global challenges of the future. Humankind's relation to a now very obviously finite natural environment, and to a social world which communicates with ever greater speed while generating more and more conflicts with regard to the content of that communication can still be illuminated by resources from German philosophy.

References

Introduction

K. Marx and F. Engels, *Werke*, Vol. 4 (Berlin: Dietz, 1956).

Chapter 1

Quotations from I. Kant are according to the standard A B pagination from the Akademie Edition, given in most editions: *Critique of Pure Reason*, B p. 132; *Foundation of the Metaphysics of Morals*, BA p. 17, BA p. 7; *Critique of Judgement*, B p. 193, A p. 190.

Chapter 2

K. Reinhold, cited in M. Bauer and D. Dahlstrom, *The Emergence of German Idealism* (Washington, DC: Catholic University of America Press, 1999), p. 62.

J. G. Herder, *Über die neuere deutsche Literatur: Fragmente* (Berlin: Aufbau, 1985), p. 373.

J. G. Hamann, *Schriften zur Sprache*, ed. Josef Simon (Frankfurt: Suhrkamp, 1967), p. 224, p. 109; *Sämtliche Werke*, 6 vols. (Vienna: Herder, 1950), Vol. 2, p. 74; Vol. 3, p. 284.

J. G. Herder, *Sprachphilosophische Schriften* (Hamburg: Meiner, 1964), p. 153.

F. D. E. Schleiermacher, *Dialektik*, ed. L. Jonas (Berlin: Reimer, 1839), p. 563.

Chapter 3

F. H. Jacobi, in H. Scholz (ed.), *Die Hauptschriften zum Pantheismusstreit zwischen Jacobi und Mendelssohn* (Berlin: Reuther and Reichard, 1916), p. 51.

J. G. Fichte, *Werke I* (Berlin: de Gruyter, 1971), p. 463; *Werke II*, p. 239.

F. W. J. Schelling, *Sämmtliche Werke*, ed. K. F. A. Schelling, I Abtheilung Vols. 1–10, II Abtheilung Bde. 1–4 (Stuttgart: Cotta, 1856–61), I/2 p. 53, I/3 p. 341, II/3 p. 7.

Chapter 4

F. Schlegel, *Kritische Schriften und Fragmente*, Studienausgabe Vols. 1–6, ed. Ernst Behler and Hans Eichner (Paderborn, Munich, Vienna, Zürich: Schöningh, 1988), Vol. 2, p. 240, p. 115; Vol. 5, p. 12; *Transcendentalphilosophie*, ed. Michael Elsässer (Hamburg: Meiner, 1991), pp. 92–3, p. 95, p. 93.

Novalis, *Werke* (Munich: Beck, 1981), p. 226, p. 181, p. 637.

F. H. Jacobi, *Jacobi an Fichte* (Hamburg: Friedrich Perthes, 1799), p. 14.

F. Schlegel, *Philosophische Lehrjahre* (1796–1828) (*Kritische Friedrich Schlegel Ausgabe*, Vol. 18) (Munich, Paderborn, Vienna: Ferdinand Schöningh, 1963), p. 518.

Chapter 5

L. Feuerbach, *Das Wesen des Christentums* (Stuttgart: Reclam, 1969), p. 400, p. 406.

K. Marx, *Ökonomisch-philosophische Manuskripte* (Leipzig: Reclam, 1970), p. 151, p. 186.

K. Marx and F. Engels, *Werke*, Vol. 13 (Berlin: Dietz, 1956 ff), pp. 8–9.

K. Marx, *Das Kapital*, Vol. 1 (Berlin: Dietz, 1975), p. 52.

Chapter 6

A. Schopenhauer, *Die Welt als Wille und Vorstellung*, in *Sämtliche Werke*, Vol. I, ed. Wolfgang Frhr. von Löhneysen (Frankfurt: Suhrkamp, 1986), p. 168; Vol. V, p. 507.

F. Nietzsche, *Sämtliche Werke. Kritische Studienausgabe* in 15 Bänden, ed. Giorgio Colli and Mazzino Montinari (Munich, Berlin,

New York: de Gruyter, 1980), Vol. 1, p. 47, p. 99, p. 100, p. 880; Vol. 6, pp. 80–1; Vol. 3, p. 467.

Chapter 7

M. Schlick, in R. Rorty (ed.), *The Linguistic Turn* (Chicago: University of Chicago Press, 1992), p. 51; cited in M. Friedman, *Reconsidering Logical Positivism* (Cambridge: Cambridge University Press, 1999), p. 29.

B. Bolzano, *Grundlegung der Logik* (Hamburg: Meiner, 1963), p. 66.

I. Kant, *Critique of Pure Reason*, B p. 172, A p. 133.

E. Husserl, *Gesammelte Schriften*, 9 vols. (Hamburg: Meiner, 1992), Vol. 8, p. 4, p. 60, p. 115, p. 36, p. 23, p. 44.

Chapter 8

E. Husserl, *Gesammelte Schriften*, 9 vols. (Hamburg: Meiner, 1992), Vol. 4, p. 666.

M. Heidegger, *Sein und Zeit* (Tübingen: Niemeyer, 1979), p. 12, p. 38; M. Heidegger, *Ursprung des Kunstwerks* (Stuttgart: Reclam, 1960), p. 62; M. Heidegger, *Zur Sache des Denkens* (Tübingen: Niemeyer, 1969), p. 63.

Chapter 9

W. Benjamin, *Gesammelte Schriften* (Frankfurt: Suhrkamp, 1980), Vol. I/3, p. 1151.

M. Horkheimer and T. Adorno, *Dialektik der Aufklärung* (Frankfurt: Fischer, 1971), p. 1, p. 5.

H.-G. Gadamer, *Wahrheit und Methode* (Tübingen: J. C. B. Mohr, 1975), p. XXVII; H.-G. Gadamer, *Ästhetik und Poetik I. Kunst als Aussage* (Tübingen: J. C. B. Mohr, 1993), p. 342.

J. Habermas, *Moralbewußtsein und kommunikatives Handeln* (Frankfurt: Suhrkamp, 1983), p. 26.

Further reading

Only English-language secondary literature on German philosophy is cited here. The basic primary texts are those discussed in each chapter: a general list would be too extensive to be useful.

General works

A. Bowie, *From Romanticism to Critical Theory: The Philosophy of German Literary Theory* (London: Routledge, 1997). Presentation of ideas concerning literature and truth from Kant and the Romantics to the Frankfurt School.

A. Bowie, *Aesthetics and Subjectivity: From Kant to Nietzsche*, 2nd edn. (Manchester: Manchester University Press, 2003). Considers the central role of aesthetics in the development of German philosophy.

A. Bowie, *Introduction to German Philosophy: From Kant to Habermas* (Cambridge: Polity, 2003). More extensive account of the issues covered in this book.

P. Gorner, *Twentieth Century German Philosophy* (Oxford: Oxford University Press, 2000). Examination of Husserl, Heidegger, Gadamer, Habermas, and Apel.

J. Habermas, *The Philosophical Discourse of Modernity* (Cambridge: Polity, 1987). Critical overview of modern philosophy by leading German philosopher.

A. O'Hear (ed.), *German Philosophy After Kant* (Cambridge: Cambridge University Press, 1999). Essays on individual philosophers and on central themes in German philosophy.

T. Pinkard, *German Philosophy 1760–1860: The Legacy of Idealism* (Cambridge: Cambridge University Press, 2002). Account of connections between philosophy and history in the period in question.

H. Schnädelbach, *Philosophy in Germany 1831–1933* (Cambridge: Cambridge University Press, 1984). Account which includes much material on lesser-known academic philosophers.

Chapter 1

H. E. Allison, *Kant's Transcendental Idealism* (New Haven, CT: Yale University Press, 1983). Defence of Kant's contentions in the *Critique of Pure Reason.*

K. Ameriks, *Interpreting Kant's Critiques* (Oxford: Clarendon Press, 2003). Essays on new approaches to the interpretation of Kant.

E. Cassirer, *Kant's Life and Thought* (New Haven, CT: Yale University Press, 1982). Biographical and philosophical account of Kant by neo-Kantian philosopher.

S. Gardner, *Routledge Philosophy Guidebook to Kant and the Critique of Pure Reason* (London: Routledge, 1999). Detailed introductory account of the first Critique.

R. Scruton, *Kant: A Very Short Introduction* (Oxford: Oxford University Press, 2001). General introduction to Kant.

P. F. Strawson, *The Bounds of Sense: An Essay on Kant's Critique of Pure Reason* (London: Routledge, 1966). Influential analytical account of Kant, which is not reliable in its interpretations of some key issues.

Chapter 2

H. Adler and W. Koepke, *A Companion to the Works of Johann Gottfried Herder* (Columbia, SC: Camden House, 2009). Essays on the main aspects of Herder's work.

I. Berlin, *The Magus of the North: J. G. Hamann and the Origins of Modern Irrationalism* (London: John Murray, 1993). Readable, but unreliable, interpretation of Hamann.

T. German, *Hamann on Language and Religion* (Oxford: Oxford University Press, 1981). Account by Hamann scholar.

J. H. Zammito, *Kant, Herder, and the Birth of Anthropology* (Chicago, IL: Chicago University Press, 2001). Contextualization of the thought of Kant and Herder in relation to often ignored issues.

Chapter 3

K. Ameriks (ed.), *The Cambridge Companion to German Idealism* (Cambridge: Cambridge University Press, 2000). Essays on the main themes and figures in German Idealism.

F. C. Beiser, *Hegel* (London: Routledge, 2005). Accessible and scholarly introduction.

F. C. Beiser, *The Fate of Reason: German Philosophy from Kant to Fichte* (Cambridge, MA: Harvard University Press, 1987). Study of the immediate reactions to Kant, dealing with many unjustly ignored philosophers.

A. Bowie, *Schelling and Modern European Philosophy* (London: Routledge, 1993). Schelling considered as a major thinker in his own right, rather than as a prelude to Hegel.

F. Neuhouser, *Fichte's Theory of Subjectivity* (Cambridge: Cambridge University Press, 1989). Lucid analytical account of Fichte's arguments.

R. B. Pippin, *Idealism as Modernism: Hegelian Variations* (Cambridge: Cambridge University Press, 1997). Philosophical essays based on the most productive contemporary interpretation of Hegel.

C. Taylor, *Hegel* (Cambridge: Cambridge University Press, 1975). Influential traditional account of Hegel's philosophy.

S. Žižek, *The Indivisible Remainder: On Schelling and Related Matters* (London: Verso, 2007). Relates Schelling to Žižek's concerns deriving from Hegel and Lacan.

Chapter 4

F. C. Beiser, *The Romantic Imperative: The Concept of Early German Romanticism* (Cambridge, MA: Harvard University Press, 2006). Scholarly but interpretatively questionable account of Romantic philosophy.

M. Frank, *The Philosophical Foundations of Early German Romanticism* (Albany, NY: SUNY Press, 2008). Reliable account by the leading scholar of early Romantic philosophy.

N. Saul, *Cambridge Companion to German Romanticism* (Cambridge: Cambridge University Press, 2009). Essays on the various philosophical and other dimensions of German Romanticism.

Chapter 5

W. Breckman, *Marx, the Young Hegelians, and the Origins of Radical Social Theory* (Cambridge: Cambridge University Press, 1999). Historical reinterpretation of the thought of the Young Hegelians.

T. Eagleton, *Marx* (London: Routledge, 1999). Assessment of Marx's philosophy from a contemporary perspective.

J. Elster, *An Introduction to Karl Marx* (Cambridge: Cambridge University Press, 1986). Analytical account of Marx.

J. Habermas, *Knowledge and Human Interests* (Cambridge: Polity, 1986). Situates Marx in a wider context of critical social theory.

K. Korsch, *Marxism and Philosophy* (London: Pluto, 1970). Influential text by leading Marxist which helped change the image of Marx's philosophy in the 1920s.

A. Schmidt, *The Concept of Nature in Marx* (New York: Schocken, 1978). Account of Marx's approaches to the question of nature.

Chapter 6

A. Bowie, *Music, Philosophy, and Modernity* (Cambridge: Cambridge University Press, 2007). Examines the importance of music for Nietzsche and other modern philosophers.

M. Clark, *Nietzsche on Truth and Philosophy* (Cambridge: Cambridge University Press, 1991). Analytical account of Nietzsche.

G. Deleuze, *Nietzsche and Philosophy* (London: Athlone, 1985). Study by major French philosopher.

C. Janaway, *Schopenhauer: A Very Short Introduction* (Oxford: Oxford University Press, 2002). Accessible historical and philosophical account of Schopenhauer.

W. Kaufmann, *Nietzsche: Philosopher, Psychologist, Antichrist* (Princeton: Princeton University Press, 1974). Clear, if uncritical, presentation of Nietzsche's ideas.

B. Magnus and K. M. Higgins (eds.), *The Cambridge Companion to Nietzsche* (Cambridge: Cambridge University Press, 1996). Collection of essays on major themes.

A. Nehamas, *Nietzsche: Life as Literature* (Cambridge: Cambridge University Press, 1987). Reinterpretation of the significance of Nietzsche.

R. Schacht, *Nietzsche* (London: Routledge, 1985). Reliable work on major themes in Nietzsche.

Chapter 7

D. Bell, *Husserl* (London: Routledge, 1990). Analytical account of Husserl.
J. A. Coffa, *The Semantic Tradition from Kant to Carnap* (Cambridge: Cambridge University Press, 1991). Historical account of the sources and early development of analytical philosophy.
M. Friedman, *Reconsidering Logical Positivism* (Cambridge: Cambridge University Press, 1999). Reinterpretations of the work of the Vienna Circle.
M. Friedman, *A Parting of the Ways: Carnap, Cassirer, and Heidegger* (Chicago, IL: Open Court, 2000). Philosophical and historical account of the contrasting analytical, neo-Kantian, and phenomenological tendencies of German philosophy.
H. Sluga, *Gottlob Frege* (London: Routledge, 1980). Historically informed study of the work of Frege.
B. Smith and D. Woodruff Smith (eds.), *The Cambridge Companion to Husserl* (Cambridge: Cambridge University Press, 1995). Volume of essays on many aspects of Husserl's work.

Chapter 8

H. L. Dreyfus, *Being-in-the-World: A Commentary on Heidegger's "Being and Time," Division I* (Cambridge, MA: MIT Press, 1991). Commentary on Heidegger's most influential work.
M. Inwood, *Heidegger: A Very Short Introduction* (Oxford: Oxford University Press, 2000). The best initial point of access to Heidegger.
C. Lafont, *Heidegger, Language, and World-Disclosure* (Cambridge: Cambridge University Press, 2000). Critical account of Heidegger on language.
S. Mulhall, *Routledge Philosophy Guidebook to Heidegger and Being and Time* (London: Routledge, 1996). Detailed introduction to *Being and Time.*
R. Safranski, *Martin Heidegger: Between Good and Evil* (Cambridge, MA: Harvard University Press, 1998). Intellectual and philosophical biography of Heidegger.

Chapter 9

S. Benhabib, *Critique, Norm and Utopia: A Study of the Foundations of Critical Theory* (New York: Columbia University Press, 1986). Philosophical study of Critical Theory.

R. Bernstein (ed.), *Habermas and Modernity* (Cambridge, MA: MIT Press, 1985). Collection of critical essays.

P. Connerton, *The Tragedy of Enlightenment: An Essay on the Frankfurt School* (Cambridge: Cambridge University Press, 1980). Study of core ideas in Critical Theory.

P. Dews (ed.), *Habermas: A Critical Reader* (Oxford: Blackwell, 1999). Collection of critical essays that approach Habermas from less familiar angles.

D. Ferris, *The Cambridge Companion to Walter Benjamin* (Cambridge: Cambridge University Press, 2004). Essays on aspects of Benjamin's thought.

R. Geuss, *The Idea of a Critical Theory* (Cambridge: Cambridge University Press, 1981). Examination of the possibility of a 'Critical Theory'.

D. Held, *Introduction to Critical Theory: Horkheimer to Habermas* (Berkeley, CA: University of California Press, 1980). Historical and theoretical account of Critical Theory.

R. Holub, *Jürgen Habermas* (London: Routledge, 1991). Study of Habermas as social critic.

M. Jay, *The Dialectical Imagination: A History of the Frankfurt School and the Institute of Social Research, 1923–1950* (Boston, MA: Little, Brown, 1973). Historical study of the development of the Frankfurt School.

G. Rose, *The Melancholy Science: An Introduction to the Thought of Theodor W. Adorno* (London: Macmillan, 1978). Study of Adorno's work.

G. Warnke, *Gadamer: Hermeneutics, Tradition and Reason* (Stanford, CA: Stanford University Press, 1987). Account of the major aspects of Gadamer's work.

Index

Bold indicates chapter on the subject.

ARISTOTLE

A Very Short Introduction

Jonathan Barnes

The influence of Aristotle, the prince of philosophers, on the intellectual history of the West is second to none. In this book Jonathan Barnes examines Aristotle's scientific research, his discoveries in logic, his metaphysical theories, his work in psychology, ethics, and politics, and his ideas about art and poetry, placing his teachings in their historical context.

> 'With compressed verve, Jonathan Barnes displays the extraordinary Versatility of Aristotle, the great systematising empiricist.'
>
> ***Sunday Times***

www.oup.co.uk/isbn/0-19-285408-9

BARTHES

A Very Short Introduction

Jonathan Culler

Roland Barthes (1915–80) was an 'incomparable enlivener of the literary mind' whose lifelong fascination was with 'the way people make their world intelligible'.

Jonathan Culler elucidates the varied theoretical contributions of this 'public experimenter' and describes the many projects which Barthes explored and which helped to change the way we think about a range of cultural phenomena, from literature, fashion, wrestling and advertising to notions of the self, of history, and of nature.

> 'The fact that Jonathan Culler has written such an excellent book . . . is in part testimony to Culler's own skills in exposition. But it is equally, if not even more so, a tribute to the very achievements he is describing; for if Barthes had been a different and more conventional figure it is doubtful whether this would have been such a good book.'
>
> **Ann Jefferson, *Times Literary Supplement***

www.oup.co.uk/isbn/0-19-280159-7

CLASSICS

A Very Short Introduction

Mary Beard and John Henderson

This Very Short Introduction to Classics links a haunting temple on a lonely mountainside to the glory of ancient Greece and the grandeur of Rome, and to Classics within modern culture – from Jefferson and Byron to Asterix and Ben-Hur.

'The authors show us that Classics is a "modern" and sexy subject. They succeed brilliantly in this regard ... nobody could fail to be informed and entertained – and the accent of the book is provocative and stimulating.'

John Godwin, *Times Literary Supplement*

'Statues and slavery, temples and tragedies, museum, marbles, and mythology – this provocative guide to the Classics demystifies its varied subject-matter while seducing the reader with the obvious enthusiasm and pleasure which mark its writing.'

Edith Hall

ONLINE CATALOGUE

A Very Short Introduction

Our online catalogue is designed to make it easy to find your ideal Very Short Introduction. View the entire collection by subject area, watch author videos, read sample chapters, and download reading guides.

http://fds.oup.com/www.oup.co.uk/general/vsi/index.html

SOCIAL MEDIA
Very Short Introduction

Join our community

www.oup.com/vsi

- Join us online at the official Very Short Introductions **Facebook** page.
- Access the thoughts and musings of our authors with our online **blog**.
- Sign up for our monthly **e-newsletter** to receive information on all new titles publishing that month.
- Browse the full range of Very Short Introductions online.
- Read **extracts** from the Introductions for free.
- Visit our library of **Reading Guides**. These guides, written by our expert authors will help you to question again, why you think what you think.
- If you are a teacher or lecturer you can order inspection copies quickly and simply via our website.